Praise for
Holding Fast

"Karen James has taken a tragic event for her and her family and used it to shine a light on the life of a man that uplifted those he touched. It's a compelling story that is sure to inspire!"

— TROY AIKMAN,
Pro Football Hall of Fame
member (2006)

"As a child living in Portland, Oregon, I could see the beautiful 11,239-foot snowcapped summit of Mount Hood from my bedroom window. I often wondered what it would be like to climb to the top. Years later when I heard the news reports that Kelly was missing on the mountain, I knew its subfreezing temperatures and eighty-mile-per-hour winds would make it a brutal place to be stranded. Kelly James was a man's man—a man of purpose. He was passionate not just about mountain climbing, but also about making his life count. When Kelly learned his church would study *The Purpose Driven Life*, he jumped at the opportunity. Without consulting Karen, he spontaneously volunteered their home to host a 40 Days of Purpose small group. When he saw a need, Kelly acted without hesitation. If you're tired of no-risk living, read this powerful story. It will grab you from the first page and won't let you go."

— RICK WARREN,
author of
The Purpose Driven Life

"In my thirty-three years of law enforcement, I have never met families like these. Something very special happened on the mountain between the rescuers and the James, Hall, and Cooke families. Karen's description of what happened on Mount Hood is the most accurate I have heard to date. With what our investigation revealed and her insight into her husband and their friend Brian Hall, she has done an amazing job of putting the pieces together. Karen's story is about mountain climbers, mountain rescue, relationships, and never giving up."

— SHERIFF JOSEPH A. WAMPLER,
Hood River County, Oregon

"Karen James's moving account of her beloved Kelly's tragic death on Mount Hood reveals how human love can transcend tragedy—even death. After losing the love of her life, Karen ironically found the perfect Love that Kelly so passionately embraced. Her touching story of tragedy, heartbreak, and ultimately, triumph will inspire you to hold fast to all those you love."

> — DENISE JACKSON,
> wife of country singer Alan
> Jackson and author of
> *It's All About Him*

"Karen James will take you on a journey you will never forget. It's an adventure and love story rolled into one with a very important life message. I remember hearing the heartbreaking news that mountain climber Kelly James had been found dead in a snow cave on Mount Hood, but I couldn't help but wonder what really happened—this is the untold story!"

> — ROGER STAUBACH,
> Pro Football Hall of Fame
> member (1985) and Executive
> Chairman, The Staubach
> Company

"Before Kelly James lost his battle on the mountaintop, he took his wife, Karen, to the moon! This is a great love story that captured the attention of our whole nation in December 2006. After the chilling pain of defeat, the reader's heart will be warmed by Karen's strength and victory."

> — RON HALL,
> author of
> *Same Kind of Different as Me*

"When Kelly was alive he watched out for Karen and the kids; now he watches over them. He went from a human being to a superbeing."

> — DENVER MOORE,
> author of
> *Same Kind of Different as Me*

"As Karen and Kelly's pastor, the news that one of our family members was missing hit us hard. Our congregation prayed and prayed that the three climbers would make it home for Christmas. While Kelly did not survive that awful storm, I am convinced he did make it *home* for Christmas. This book will tell you not only what happened on the mountain but, more important, what happened in the lives of so many who roped their lives together during and after the tragedy. My prayer is that this inspirational story will deeply touch and help motivate others to keep their eyes on the true summit!"

— Gary Brandenburg,
Senior Pastor,
Fellowship Bible Church, Dallas

"This is an inspiring personal and heartfelt look at the tragic climbing trip on Mount Hood that took the life of Karen's husband and his two climbing partners in December 2006. From the moment she received the first phone call indicating there was trouble on the mountain, Karen James tells the story of her family, her husband, and the rescue efforts that captured the attention of the media. Karen takes the reader into her life and not only retraces the family bonds and personal experiences that have kept her looking forward, but also pieces together the details of the climb that likely led to her husband's death on Mount Hood."

—Dave Waag,
Hood River Crag Rats

"Karen's description of the December 2006 Mount Hood tragedy is the most detailed and inspiring I have heard. Karen provides an intimate and behind-the-scenes view of what transpired on the mountain and what her family had to endure. This is a heroic tale of a climb gone terribly wrong and how a family and its faith can survive the worst of catastrophes."

— Steve Rollins,
Rescue Leader,
Portland Mountain Rescue

HOLDING FAST

The Untold Story of the Mount Hood Tragedy

Karen James

THOMAS NELSON
Since 1798

NASHVILLE   DALLAS   MEXICO CITY   RIO DE JANEIRO   BEIJING

Published in Nashville, Tennessee, by Thomas Nelson. Thomas Nelson is a registered trademark of Thomas Nelson, Inc.

Published in association with The Idea Agency and Rosenbaum & Associates Literary Agency, Brentwood, Tennessee.

Thomas Nelson, Inc., titles may be purchased in bulk for educational, business, fund-raising, or sales promotional use. For information, please e-mail SpecialMarkets@ThomasNelson.com.

Unless otherwise noted, Scripture quotations are taken from the HOLY BIBLE: NEW INTERNATIONAL VERSION®. © 1973, 1978, 1984 by International Bible Society. Used by permission of Zondervan Publishing House. All rights reserved.

Library of Congress Cataloging-in-Publication Data

James, Karen, 1963–
    Holding fast : the untold story of the Mount Hood tragedy / Karen James.
        p. cm.
    ISBN 978-1-59555-343-0
    1. Mountaineering accidents—Oregon—Hood, Mount. 2. James, Kelly.
    3. Mountaineers—United States—Biography. 4. James, Karen, 1963– I. Title.
GV199.92.H64J36 2008
796.52209795'61—dc22   2008031654

Printed in the United States of America

09 10 11 12 QW 5 4 3

To the love of my life, Kelly James,

thank you for taking me to the moon and back.

Love Forever, Karen

I can do all things through Him who strengthens me.

—Philippians 4:13

Hold Fast

To everyone who's hurting
To those who've had enough
To all the undeserving
That should cover all of us
Please do not let go
I promise there is hope
Hold fast
Help is on the way
Hold fast
He's come to save the day
What I've learned in my life
One thing greater than my strife
Is His grasp
So hold fast

Will this season ever pass?
Can we stop this ride?
Will we see the sun at last?
Or could this be our lot in life?
Please do not let go
I promise you there's hope

You may think you're all alone
And there's no way that anyone could know
What you're going through
But if you only hear one thing
Just understand that we are all the same
Searching for the truth

The truth of what we're soon to face

Unless someone comes to take our place

Is there anyone?

All we want is to be free

Free from our captivity, Lord

Here He comes

Contents

Prologue

DRIVEN BY THE PASSION OF ADVENTURE AND THE MOUNTAINS' MAJESTIC beauty, a successful architect named George William Barrett left his home in England in 1906 to climb in the Canadian Rockies. He would never return home and tell the story of his great climb and trip to the summit. On that ill-fated trip, Barrett died in a climbing accident, very far from home, leaving behind a loving wife and six children. He was my great-grandfather. I did not learn the circumstances of his death until after I married Kelly.

Deep inside, I knew that there could be no coincidence that exactly one hundred years later, my landscape architect and avid mountain climber husband was also in trouble on a mountain. Of the many prayers I prayed through the long days and nights while we searched for Kelly, Brian, and Nikko on Mount Hood, I asked God not to repeat my family history.

Tragically, Kelly and my great-grandfather shared the same fate, but I made a commitment to myself that my life would be very different from that of my great-grandmother. According to my grandmother, shortly after my great-grandfather's death, her mother died of a "broken heart." Although my heart, like hers, was broken, I instinctively knew that through my faith, I would be given the strength to carry on and live without the greatest love of my life.

My great-grandfather George William Barrett (*standing, second row from the top, cigar in mouth*) died in a mountain-climbing accident four years after this photograph was taken. My great-grandmother (*on his right*) died of a broken heart six months after his death.

PART 1

The Man Behind the Headlines

ONE

Two Miles High

AS KELLY JAMES LAY ALONE IN A SNOW CAVE NEARLY ELEVEN THOUSAND feet high on Mount Hood, he wondered, *Where the h— is Brian? Come on, dude.* His climbing partner, Brian Hall, and fellow climber Jerry "Nikko" Cooke had left Kelly a few days earlier to descend the mountain in search of help. It was December, and Kelly was stuck on a mountain in Oregon, far from his home in Dallas, Texas. What had started as a quick weekend trip to practice ice climbing in preparation for tackling Mount Everest had turned into a life-and-death situation unlike any that Kelly had ever faced. He was a veteran mountaineer, and he kept replaying the decisions and events of the climb in his head.

Kelly reached for his cell phone. *Please let me talk to Karen.* Kelly dialed and tried to reach his wife, but there was no signal. *All right, I'll try 911.* Kelly dialed, but again there was no signal. By that time he was so wet, weak, and tired, he did not have the energy to venture out of the snow cave and try to get a better signal. A vicious storm was raging, and even if he was strong enough, he had little hope of going anywhere to pick up a stronger signal. *Just need to sit tight. Brian knows where I am,* thought Kelly.

Glancing toward the cave's entrance, he could see that it was almost covered over from the recent snowfall. The climbers built this cave to seek shelter from the brutal weather. They started the trip together, but now Kelly was separated from his two buddies. Alone in the cave, he tried not to focus on the pain in his shoulder and legs. Kelly thought, *I need to dig out the snow covering the entrance.* But Brian and Nikko had the snow shovel with them. *Could I even use it?* he questioned himself. Kelly could no longer feel his feet. This was a first for Kelly, who was used to being in top shape. He had natural physical strength and endurance that amazed his friends and family.

Something had gone terribly wrong just below the summit. In the middle of December, Mount Hood can be just as cruel as Everest, and despite their careful planning, the trio could not escape Mother Nature's fury. On the north face of Mount Hood, there is nowhere to go but up, due to the extreme danger of down climbing the ice. The plan was simple enough. Go up, over the top, and descend the south side. But it didn't happen that way.

As Kelly reflected on their dire situation, his mind constantly raced back to his family. He knew they had to be trying to call him, especially his wife, Karen. No matter where he was in the world, he and Karen had a pact that every night each of them would reach out and call to say good night. Throughout their marriage, the only time they missed saying, "I love you," before bedtime was when Kelly could not get cell phone reception on a mountain. The longest he had ever been without talking to Karen was five days on Mount McKinley, when he and Brian were caught in their tent in a whiteout.

I wish I was home. Don't worry, man. You'll get there, he reassured himself. Kelly's natural optimistic disposition had always served him well in difficult times. He was a big believer in mind over matter. Despite his worsening condition, he continued to think, *It's just a matter of time until help comes.* His positive attitude would not allow his mind to travel to the dark place that perhaps Brian and Nikko never made it down the mountain.

As the most experienced climber of the group, Kelly wished he was with them. Before they separated, he told them, "Put in extra protection and be super-safe." Kelly was referring to the climbing tactic of putting screws in the ice to secure the climbing rope. The more ice screws, the more protection. Even though they are roped together, if one climber falls, it is impossible for the remaining climber to stay on the mountain just holding on to his ice tools embedded into the face of the mountain. The jolt of a falling climber and his body weight can quickly pluck the other climbers off the mountain. In dangerous areas, climbers need to secure, at intervals, their ropes attached to ice screws, so if one falls, they will fall only the distance of the last embedded ice screw and not thousands of feet to their deaths.

They should have been back by now. But weather conditions were horrible, and he figured that the guys must be hunkered down in another snow cave waiting for the storm to break.

One of the worst storms in a decade had bombarded the mountain for a week, dumping up to five feet of new snow, bringing wind chills estimated at around forty degrees below zero.

Despite the strength and size of all three men, they were no match for the storm. The hurricane-strength winds, with gusts up to 130 miles per hour, had rendered them helpless.

Nevertheless, they had persevered and were able to seek shelter in the snow cave. Kelly reassured himself, *That's it. The weather is the only logical reason why they haven't made it back yet. Just hurry, guys.*

As an experienced climber, Kelly was well aware of what was happening to his body. He had hypothermia, and he understood the physical symptoms and

Veteran mountain climber Kelly James at the age of forty-eight.

progression of the condition. *No matter what, I will not undress,* he reminded himself. Kelly was thinking about a bizarre condition linked with hypothermia called paradoxical undressing; thinking that they are hot, victims start removing their clothing. In the past, he had told Karen stories about this condition when they discussed the dangers of climbing. But Kelly never really thought it would happen to him. After all, he was a pro at getting out of tight situations. In his forty-eight years of life, he had never met a mountain he couldn't tackle.

He dismissed the thought of hypothermia, and his confidence grew again. He would make it out of this snow cave, and he would beat the hypothermia because he had the strength and presence of mind to fight off the bizarre undressing condition. After all, he thought, *God will protect me.*

As the minutes stretched into hours, his shivering became more violent, and when he tried to talk, he could tell his speech was sluggish. For the first time, he wasn't sure how much longer he could fight off the bitter cold. Outside the cave, the temperature had dropped into the teens with wind gusts up to one hundred miles per hour, resulting in a deadly below-zero double-digit wind chill. A snow cave can serve as good protection from a storm, but in such severe weather, Kelly needed his small portable stove to boil water and a sleeping bag to escape his wet clothes that were speeding up the hypothermia. At that point, he was separated from his important gear that he had so carefully laid out to pack on his living room floor in Dallas only a few days earlier.

His body was starting to shut down. But most upsetting of all, he was unable to disguise it in his voice, and he was aware that Karen knew that something was very wrong.

As he thought back to the last time they spoke—he couldn't quite remember when it happened—he had no doubt that his prayers were answered. Making several attempts to call out, he received no signal each time. Kelly had given up trying to reach Karen and 911. Then on Sunday afternoon as he lay in the snow cave, he heard a sound. At first, he thought he was dreaming, and then he realized that his phone was ringing. He fumbled to answer the call but missed it.

Looking down at the phone, he saw that his oldest son, Jason, had just called. Kelly used every bit of coordination he had left to redial, and as he heard the phone ringing, he repeated, "Please! Please!" Jason picked up.

Relief swept over Kelly as Jason answered. Then Ford, his second oldest son, took the phone from his brother and started to ask questions. Kelly told the two boys everything he could think of to help the rescue workers find him. Despite his deteriorating condition, his mind was still strong, and he knew he could depend on them.

Then Karen got on the phone. Unlike the boys' loud voices and rapid-fire series of search and rescue questions, Karen's voice was soft. He could hear it crack as she said, "Hi, honey." At that moment, both of them knew this was a conversation like none before. In the brief exchange, their souls connected. Their hearts were speaking to each other without either one of them uttering a word. They talked a couple of minutes and exchanged "I love you's." But Kelly realized it was what Karen had not asked him that made the biggest impact. For the first time she did not ask, "When will you be down off the mountain?"

After hanging up, he whispered, "I'm sorry, baby." Reassured by knowing that the boys were with her, he wondered, *Where are my other two kids, Katie and Jack?* Kelly's heart ached. *Please, God, don't take me yet. They need me.*

His thoughts flashed to the weekend before his trip when he was with his mother, Lou Ann, tiling her kitchen floor. *You can't do this to my mom. She's already had such a tough life. She'll be crushed. Just give me some more time with her and my brothers and sisters.*

Kelly's mind was then still. God had rescued him from other tight spots, but instinctively he knew this time would be different. The thought that he might be leaving his family brought deep sorrow, and he wept, knowing what he was leaving behind. *It was just a quick weekend trip. Christmas is in two weeks. It wasn't supposed to turn out like this.*

Then in true Kelly James style, he refocused, and everything he believed to be true in his life came full force into his heart and mind. He turned his eyes away from this earth and focused all his attention on God.

Throughout his stay in the snow cave, Kelly never felt alone because he knew he wasn't. For him, God and the mountains were inseparable. He felt closest to God when he climbed, and this was truly the closest he had been to death.

Kelly was not afraid of dying. To Karen's amazement, he often expressed his excitement about what heaven would be like. There was never any doubt in his mind about what would happen to him after death. Kelly believed that when it was his time, nothing any person could do would change this fact. This sense of peace and confidence in his ultimate destination, combined with his passion for life, drew people to him.

With his earthly body failing him, Kelly realized this would not be another climbing story that he and Brian would tell while popping a cold beer on his patio at home. He thought about Brian, *Man, you have got to watch out for them.* As with many climbers, there was an understanding between them that if one died, the other would be there for his family. Kelly knew beyond a shadow of a doubt that Brian would do this for him.

While trapped on Mount Hood, Kelly was holding fast to his spiritual beliefs and never gave up thinking that help was on the way. What he understood was that instead of being saved by rescuers, he would soon experience the most incredible rescue of all. It was time to surrender his earthly body. But Kelly had to do one more thing for his family before he died. Lying there on the cold, snowy floor with his head resting on his pack, he removed his right glove, extended his arm, and curled back all fingers except his ring finger with his signet JKJ ring prominently displayed. In his last dying moments, Kelly wanted to send a signal to his family. It would be his last act of love for them, and it would be his final "I love you"—at least on this earth.

AS KELLY'S WIFE, I BELIEVE THAT I KNEW IN MY HEART HOW HE SPENT his final minutes, hours, and days. I spent many nights lying awake, imagining what he had to endure, both mentally and physically, in the fight for his life against the sub-zero-degree temperatures. In the months following his death, I did not have all the facts surrounding his death, yet the answers to what happened seemed strangely within my grasp. I attributed this to my belief that even in death, God had not severed our bond of love. Over the course of the next year, I learned details, unreleased publicly, surrounding the tragedy that confirmed my initial thoughts. But most amazingly, I took a journey that revealed the presence of God in my life and my husband's life and showed me how love transcends death.

TWO

A Tough Beginning

"PLEASE, DADDY, DON'T KILL MOMMY!"

With his hands tightly around her throat Lou Ann was able to get enough air to plead for her life. "Jess, please stop it!" This wasn't the first time her husband had tried to strangle her and had choked her into unconsciousness.

At that point the children were crying. Lou Ann kept gasping for breath, struggling to break his grip. At 110 pounds she was no match for the 220-pound physically fit former star athlete. He violently pushed her down to the floor, and just as quickly as it started, it was over. Jess walked away, mumbling under his breath.

Lou Ann rushed to comfort the children, and she started to cry. Many times she and the boys were able to escape the abuse by running out to their car and hiding all night behind a nearby barn until Jess sobered up and left the house the next morning for work. But this time they were not so lucky.

Lou Ann and her four little boys were caught in a trap of domestic violence, but they had virtually no resources to help protect them. In the late 1950s, law enforcement and the legal system were male dominated. Many people believed that domestic violence was better kept behind closed doors. Back then it was considered a family issue and no one else's business.

At age twenty-seven, Lou Ann had already seen her life come crashing down around her. She would not have the fairy-tale ending that she had dreamed of as a little girl. Her only goal now was to protect her children from the man she once thought would protect and cherish her.

When eighteen-year-old Lou Ann Sharpless saw Frank Allison James II

Lou Ann Sharpless
at age eighteen in 1951.

walk across campus, she was starstruck. Tall and handsome, he played football at the University of Houston. Jess, as his friends affectionately called him, was the big man on campus and was well known for many years after his college days as holding the record for blocking the most punts at the university. On campus he had his pick of girls. One day, a stunning brunette caught his attention. Jess approached her, and Lou Ann's heart skipped a beat when such a catch as Jess expressed an interest in her. He swept her off her feet.

At age nineteen, Lou Ann married Jess James; he was kind, loving, and everything she dreamed her Prince Charming would be. They stayed in Houston and started a family. Together they had four boys. Frank Allison James III was their firstborn, followed by Fredrick David and Thomas Benny. Their youngest, Jeffrey Kelly James, was born on Groundhog Day, February 2, 1958.

Shortly before Frank's birth, Jess was recruited to go out to Los Angeles and play football for the LA Rams. But his dream of being a big football star collapsed after he was injured in training camp and was forced to return to Texas. Back home in the Lone Star state his new job was far from the glamorous role of a professional football player. Instead of looking forward to being greeted by large cheering crowds, each morning he faced a large barren field dotted with oil derricks. He was assigned to repairing and assembling equipment pumping Texas crude.

Lou Ann witnessed Jess seeking relief for his shattered dream in the bottom of a bottle, which eventually resulted in the loss of his oil field job. During this time, she saw him take out his frustration and anger on her, and their marriage steadily went from bad to worse. Over the next few years, Lou Ann hoped and prayed that things would get better. Sometimes they did, but the lure of the bottle always appeared to be too powerful. Finally in

Jess James playing football in 1951.

1960, now fearing for her life and the safety of her children, she decided to make a run for it to escape the physical abuse. Although Jess had not hurt the kids, she was fearful that when they were old enough to defend her, they too might be in striking range. With only eight hundred dollars to her name, she loaded up her 1949 DeSoto with four sleepy little boys, ranging in age from seven to two. Glancing at Houston in her rearview mirror, she prayed that her troubles were behind her. But that was not to be.

Lou Ann set out for Dallas in an attempt to hide in the big, bustling city, and she was fortunate enough to find a job the second day in town. She went straight to work, often juggling up to three jobs at a time to make ends meet. Barely able to support the family, she and the boys moved into low-income housing called the projects

The four James brothers (*left to right*), Frank, Kelly, Benny, and Fred, in 1963.

13

near Baylor Hospital. She took a job there because it was within walking distance. Then her worst nightmare happened. Unbeknownst to Lou Ann, Jess had hired a private detective to find her. Lou Ann believed that Jess's loss of control and anger toward her drove him to take away what she loved the most. While she was at work, Jess made his move to kidnap the children. Frank, being the oldest, was able to escape. The three younger boys were no match for the former football player, however, and he easily rounded them up and took them back to his small hometown in the Texas hill country.

Lou Ann was beside herself at the loss of her three boys. She immediately sent Frank to hide at her elderly widowed mother's home in Arkansas because she thought it was only a matter of time until Jess would try to get him too. He would be safe outside Dallas. Realizing that her mother could not financially support them, she was forced to remain in Dallas and work, sending money to her mother to take care of Frank for a few months until she could find a way to get her other boys back.

There appeared to be nowhere in the legal system to turn for help. Based on her prior experience, Lou Ann believed that the local officials in Jess's hometown would never help her. The good old boy network was stronger than ever, and a woman like Lou Ann never stood a chance.

Every morning and night she prayed to find a way to get her boys back. Her opportunity came one night when working the evening shift. Jess showed up at the hospital looking for her, and he was carrying a knife. Terrified, she hid in the basement until law enforcement arrived. Jess was arrested for having an open knife and was taken to jail.

She had waited almost three months for this day, and she had to act fast. While he was in jail, Lou Ann made the 150-mile trip to Jess's hometown in her old decrepit car, now missing the reverse gear, determined to get her boys. They were at Jess's father's house, and once there, Lou Ann demanded them. They ran out and jumped in the car, and she hit the gas as hard as the pedal would go and drove to Arkansas to reunite the younger boys with Frank. When the four little boys saw each other, there were hugs, kisses, and laughs all around. The James brothers were together again, and Lou Ann intended to keep it that way.

She temporarily left the boys with her mother for safekeeping, but she knew they needed to be with her. Jess was still harassing her, though, and she could not escape his abusive grip.

After facing law enforcement and a legal system that didn't seem to care, Lou Ann decided to try one more time. She called the Dallas district attorney's office and was shocked to hear a female assistant district attorney on the other end of the phone. It was the first time she had ever talked to a woman in a position of authority, and it was the first time anyone in the system was willing to help her. The assistant DA put out a warrant for Jess's arrest, and Lou Ann was able to bring the boys back to Dallas and try to rebuild her life.

Her grueling work schedule was unbearable at times, yet Lou Ann had no choice—and she was determined to provide for her boys. Even though she worked around the clock, Kelly never forgot the tight rein she kept on her boys and the healthy fear of discipline she instilled in them. Later in life Kelly affectionately remembered Sunday mornings and said that even though his mother was coming off a late shift and trying to catch a few precious hours of sleep, she made sure the boys got up and went to church.

In spite of their tough financial situation, Lou Ann kept her boys together and out of harm's way. Her boys were true blessings, and she was convinced that they would grow up one day to be very special men.

The four boys were inseparable, and despite their constant teasing and rough play, they deeply loved each other. They all knew how to throw a punch, and the other kids soon learned that when you messed with one James brother, get ready, because you usually had to deal with three more.

The uncertainty of living hand to mouth changed in 1969 when Lou Ann married Logan Cameron, and the boys gained a stepfather and two stepsisters, Carol and Betsy. Not long after the marriage, they also got a new baby sister named Traci, who quickly stole the hearts of all the James brothers.

They now had a nice house to live in, but all was not well. The demon of alcohol abuse took its toll on the family. Logan eventually beat the alcohol and stopped drinking, but the effects made an impact.

Even though Kelly's childhood was far from ideal, he never grew up seeing the glass half empty. He had the unique ability to acknowledge the bad times, hold people responsible for their actions, learn from mistakes, and always see a big, beautiful rainbow after a storm. This attitude even extended to his father. After Jess and Lou Ann's divorce, under court order, the boys saw their father during the summers. Over the years, while Kelly remembered the negative, it did not affect his ability to love and hold on to the good times. He was able to develop a guarded but loving relationship with his father. Kelly would remark, "Despite everything that happened, I still love my Dad and miss him. We did have our share of good times together." At times Lou Ann just shook her head in disbelief when Kelly told her, "But, Mom, I had a great childhood," and she knew he meant it.

Kelly claimed few traits from his biological father, yet he greatly appreciated his father's natural athletic ability. All four of the James brothers had impressive athletic ability. As the oldest, Frank led the pack as a gifted football player, and Kelly, the youngest, achieved a stellar record as captain of his wrestling team at Lake Highlands High School in Dallas, Texas.

These two brothers were united by more than just their blood and athletic ability; both gained a love for God at a very young age. When most adolescent boys were solely focused on girls and sports, Frank and Kelly had an unexplainable passion for an additional topic that would affect them for the rest of their lives. For them faith was not reserved just for Sundays, and they regularly stayed up late into the night and debated theology, in a most adult way. Kelly reflected fondly on these talks of God when he spoke about his special relationship with Frank, and their relationship deepened through their school years. When it was time to choose a college, Kelly followed in his older brother's footsteps and attended Texas Tech University.

After Texas Tech, Frank was awarded the D.Phil. in history from Oxford

University and a Ph.D. in theology from Westminster Theological Seminary in Pennsylvania. He would go on to become the president of Reformed Theological Seminary in Orlando, Florida, and serve as professor of systematic and historical theology. Unlike his brother, Kelly took less of an academic route, but nonetheless, his search to understand and learn more about his faith was comparable in a very different way. For the youngest James brother, understanding God was as simple as standing on a mountain, and so his passion was born. Their lives took different paths, but they ended their journey the same way it started, with a common love for God and the big brother looking out for the youngest.

Kelly (*right*) with his sister, Traci, and brother Frank in 1987.

THREE

Our Adventure Begins

IT WAS A FEW DAYS BEFORE CHRISTMAS IN 1997 WHEN MY BEST FRIEND, Kathleen McDonald Jacobson, asked me to join her and her husband, Jake, at a Christmas party. I could tell Kathleen was up to something. She men-

tioned that her landscape architect, affectionately known as Tarzan, would also be attending. I was getting my life together after breaking away from a very painful relationship, and just like any true girlfriend, Kathleen was playing matchmaker, determined to find Mr. Right for me.

When I saw Kelly James walk through the door, I had to smile. It was hard to miss the man. His shoulder-length brown hair, twinkling hazel eyes, and bright blue jacket made him quite noticeable in the conservative crowd.

Me and my friends Jon "Jake" Jacobson (*left*) and Kathleen Jacobson (*right*).

19

Almost immediately I said to myself, *Cute. Yes. But not for me.*

Kelly looked a bit too "bad boy," and I had made a decision a while back to steer clear of that type. Despite my reservations, we entered into a conversation, and he told me about his day playing paintball with his children. I learned very quickly about his four wonderful children: Jason, the artist and thinker; Ford, the missionary and athlete; Katie, his beautiful princess; and Jack, a blessing from heaven.

In the middle of his paintball story, Kelly suddenly looked embarrassed as he motioned to the side of his face and said it was swollen because one of the kids had shot him. While I had not noticed the mark on his face, it didn't take me long to know that my first impression was wrong and I was staring directly into the eyes of a very good guy.

After one date, Kelly and I were inseparable. As we looked back and talked about our courtship, we realized that we had met at the perfect time. Kelly had married very young and was divorced when we met. He wore his heart on his sleeve and shared with me how he had spent the last few years picking up the pieces of his life. During this time, Kelly had grown spiritually and emotionally, and he was now busy spending time with his four children and running his own business as a landscape architect. He had already experienced his share of heartache, as had I. Unaware of each other's prayers, both of us had been asking for direction, and to our amazement, we had been directed straight into each other's arms.

Being with Kelly was like nothing I had ever experienced. He had a passion for life and a love for people that were contagious. I found myself doing things I had never dreamed of, and the biggest surprise of all was mountaineering. Close to two months after we started dating, Kelly asked me to join him camping. He was about to turn forty and wanted to spend this special birthday on a mountain. I had never been camping before, and the idea of a mountain birthday party sounded like great fun. The fact that it was February and we were going to Mount Wheeler in New Mexico should have been my first clue that it would not be a typical camping trip or birthday celebration.

Prior to the trip, Kelly took me to REI, an outdoor gear and equipment store, and helped me pick out some boots and clothing that claimed to wick away the perspiration. I wasn't quite sure why I needed them since I seemed to be doing quite fine all my life without wick-enabled clothing, but he sounded convincing, so I agreed. Kelly handed me a checklist of a few more items to bring and said, "That's it. It's all you will need." He then added, "Oh, and make sure you work out extra hard to get ready."

In a couple of weeks, we arrived with great anticipation at the mountain. I looked around and asked, "So where are we camping?"

Kelly pointed and said, "Up there." I took a deep breath and swallowed hard as I realized I needed about two extra months on the StairMaster at the gym before I would be ready to do this climb. Kelly did not seem to notice my lengthy pause or lack of excitement, and he went into action. Because I did not have my own backpack, he strapped one of his extra packs on my back and said, "Let's go."

The physical nature of the climb was much harder than I had anticipated. In some areas the snow was up to our knees, and I found the constant motion of lifting up my feet to punch through it exhausting. Determined to impress my new beau, I just kept moving and falling farther behind Kelly. I guess I must have been quite the sight because I remember Kelly turning around and bursting out in laughter. To my relief, he quickly whipped out a pair of snowshoes from his backpack and walked toward me to strap them on my feet. Kelly said, "I guess I should have thought about this early on." I decided to keep my comments to myself and just smiled.

Since this was my first time on a climb, I was ill equipped for the outdoors. I quickly learned that my fashion parka trimmed in faux fur, along with my makeup and the other beauty necessities I had sneaked into the pack while Kelly wasn't looking, were definitely not practical. I also understood why Kelly had talked extensively about "packing light." It seemed that the longer we climbed, the heavier my pack became. At one point I could not go any farther and asked Kelly if we could take a break. Without hesitation, he stopped and helped me take the backpack off. He unzipped my pack and reached in to get a protein bar for me. He then stopped and looked at me with complete bewilderment as he pulled out my butane cordless curling iron. "Karen, why is there a curling iron in the backpack?" A little embarrassed, I just tilted my head and smiled. That was all the explanation Kelly needed. He shook his head, smiled back, and muttered something under his breath.

As we continued to climb, I followed him, careful to step exactly in his footsteps to save energy since he was doing all the work by breaking the trail in the snow. The view helped me forget the heavy pack and strenuous activity. The snow-covered mountain with the birds soaring above was breathtaking. It was so quiet and serene. I had never seen or experienced anything like it.

Kelly and me on Mount Wheeler.

After a day of climbing, we reached the top and started back down to pitch our tent midway on the mountain. As the sun set, the temperature quickly dropped, and I became concerned that we would actually be sleeping in temperatures well below freezing. I naïvely took comfort in the fact that I had a couple of hand warmers in my parka left over from my last ski trip and wondered if they could prevent frostbite.

Fortunately, just as I started doubting the wisdom of climbing a mountain in February, he said, "I've got a surprise."

From his backpack, Kelly pulled out a bottle of wine and a CD player, and we toasted his birthday. With the stars shining brightly above, he put in a Jimmy LaFave CD and played "Walk Away Renee." That night we danced on the mountain, and it was the first time he said, "I love you."

Throughout our marriage, he told me that it was the most romantic night of his life. We often repeated that special moment by turning down the lights and dancing to the same song in our living room.

On that trip with Kelly, I started to learn about his love for the mountains and climbing. He began climbing while he was in college, and from that point it became a passion that stirred his soul. Throughout his life, the mountains called to him to strap on his backpack and venture out for a climb even more challenging than the last.

Climbing was serious business for Kelly, and he was a serious climber. He studied and practiced the sport with a personal commitment to be the best he could be. This drive led him to climb and summit some of the most revered mountains for climbers: Mount McKinley, the Eiger, and Alpamayo, along with other impressive peaks in the Alps and Andes. Kelly had also guided dozens of climbing trips for family and friends on Mount Rainier, in Washington.

If Kelly wasn't on a mountain, he was always looking for ways to improvise and brush up on his technique. One year, he spent his lunch hours climbing

© Dallas Morning News

This photo of Kelly climbing the side of a bridge appeared in the *Dallas Morning News* on June 6, 1992.

23

a stone wall next to a Dallas bridge. The sight of Kelly scaling the wall caught the attention of a *Dallas Morning News* photographer driving by one day. She stopped and asked Kelly if she could take his picture. He agreed, but only on the condition that she did not reveal the location of the bridge because he feared that city officials would shut down his lunch hour pastime.

The next morning, there was Kelly on the front page of the metro section, and the location of his secret climbing spot was revealed. Immediately Kelly called the photographer to ask why she named the location. The photographer apologized and said it was done after she turned in the photo. Needless to say, he had to look for another lunch hour adventure.

Some people might have considered him just an extreme sportsman, but he was multidimensional and a Renaissance man. He was very good at many things. Kelly wrote wonderful poetry, designed incredible architectural outdoor features, and was a talented carpenter. He was extremely physically and mentally strong, and yet he was one of the most sensitive and romantic men I have ever met.

WHILE HE HAD A LOVE FOR CLIMBING, HIS PASSION EXTENDED TO HIS children and me. Through poetry, love letters, and heart-to-heart talks, he made sure that we knew he loved and cherished us. (At the end of this book, I have included some of his poems and letters to me.) Kelly often worked to merge all his passions, and the kids and I knew that his need to climb was essential to his being.

He took the merging of his passions to the ultimate heights when he proposed to me on Mount Rainier. I had joined him and three of his friends—Sean McCarthy, Mark Oehlschlaeger, and John McWhinney. Kelly was so happy to have me along for the trip and kept referring to it as the adventure of my life. I trained for months, and it was the most physically challenging feat I had attempted.

Kelly had climbed Mount Rainier, which rises more than 14,400 feet, more than twenty times, and now he wanted me to have the same experience. On this trip, I learned the basics of mountaineering, such as how to self-arrest and stop myself with an ice axe if I was falling. I experienced the helpless feeling of hearing the sound of a nearby avalanche.

It was a two-day climb. On the first day we crossed the glacier, roping up together, and then proceeded up the mountain until we reached our first campsite around 7,800 feet. On the second day we headed out at 4:00 a.m. in an attempt to get to the summit and then back down to our camp before afternoon. As we climbed in the predawn darkness, with only our headlamps to guide the way, I thought, *This is* not *fun*. Unlike Kelly, who was in his element, I did not have the same appreciation for being out in the freezing morning hours on the side of a mountain. It was cold, scary, and incredibly hard.

Kelly looked back, and I guess he could sense my discouragement. He smiled and said, "Don't worry. You are doing great! When the sun comes up, your spirits will rise. I promise."

As dawn started to break, I could see how far we had climbed. The view was breathtaking, and I had a completely different take on the experience. It was incredible.

As we climbed closer to the summit, Kelly decided to stop at an area called Camp Hazard located at approximately 11,600 feet. He wanted to assess the situation and evaluate our bid for the summit. At this point, Kelly changed his mind and decided a summit attempt would be a bad idea for the majority of the group. He told us, "I am turning everyone back, except John. It's getting late, and we're going too slow. If I don't do this, we are going to get caught on top when the bad weather comes in, and we'll have to build a snow cave." Kelly was keeping a close eye on the weather and carefully watching the clouds in the distance.

Looking back, I realize I had summit fever because when Kelly told me I could not go on, all I wanted to do was to reach the top. The fact that I didn't care about the danger shocked me because it was totally out of my safety-conscious character.

As Kelly and John climbed on, we made our way down to the lower campsite. I told myself, *I'm never talking to him again!* Sensing my frustration, Sean, a psychiatrist by profession, decided to help me through this moment. Years later, Kelly, Sean, and I would affectionately remember this time and laugh at Sean's impromptu counseling session climbing down Mount Rainier.

We finally returned to our campsite, and Kelly and John joined us a couple of hours later, all pumped up about reaching the summit.

Kelly proposing to me atop Mount Rainier in 1999.

I was sitting in my tent, and Kelly popped his head in and said, "Come out."

I turned away and said, "No, I'm mad at you because you wouldn't let me go to the summit."

Kelly let out a big laugh that made me madder. "Come on. I've got something to cheer you up," he said.

Curious and bored with sitting in the tent, I reluctantly came out. I then mumbled, "Nothing is going to cheer me up."

Kelly replied, "I bet this will."

All of a sudden on the snow-covered mountain, Kelly got down on his knees and said, "What are you doing the rest of your life?" and pulled out an engagement ring from his jacket pocket. Kelly didn't have to ask the question, "Will you marry me?" It was clear what he meant.

Without hesitation I said, "Yes," and started to cry.

His proposal was a complete surprise. Although we had been dating more than a year and were definitely a committed couple, I never spoke of marriage. Not because I wasn't interested, but because I wanted this free-spirited mountain man to come to the realization on his own that he could not live without me. I already knew that I could not live without him.

In addition to taking me to the perfect setting, Kelly seemed to have thought of every detail. He intentionally had his close friends along on the trip to share in one of his life's greatest memories, and he made sure that they were ready with a camera to capture a candid picture we would cherish. I had reached the emotional summit of my life, and the physical one I just left behind paled in comparison.

David Bateman Photography

Our wedding. *Left to right:* Katie, me, Kelly, Jack, Jason, and Ford.

Back home, I called everyone to share my news. The moment was sweetened when I learned that in addition to getting my parents' blessing, he had asked his kids for their permission to marry me. Kelly's love for his kids and desire for us to become a strong family unit touched me greatly and deepened my respect for him. With the kids standing by our sides we were married at our church on September 30, 2000. More than seventy-five of our closest friends and family members witnessed our "I do's." Together we set off to build a life that dreams are made of.

KELLY ALWAYS INVOLVED US IN HIS CLIMBING, BOTH PHYSICALLY AND emotionally. Whether it was planning a trip or telling the stories of the summit, he made us feel a part of his adventures. Shortly after we were married, he was looking for a new climbing partner because his former partner had moved away and stopped climbing. Kelly knew the qualities and skills it took to successfully climb a mountain and get back down safely. A good climbing partner watches your back and can mean the difference between success and failure, life and death. Kelly took me along on the "get to know you" dinners and afterward quizzed me for my thoughts about the climbing partner candidates.

After meeting a couple of climbers, I told Kelly the same thing: "He's not the one. I know he would cut the rope too fast."

Kelly and Brian Hall in Colorado in 2006.

I was referring to the dilemma that climbers face when they are roped up together and one falls. In some cases, they must make a split-second decision to cut the rope below them and let the climber fall, or they themselves will also be pulled off the mountain. I wanted to make sure that the man Kelly selected as a partner would do everything in his power to save my husband before cutting the rope. That man would turn out to be Brian Hall.

When I first met Brian, I knew immediately that he was the right climbing partner for Kelly. He was a personal trainer and the perfect specimen of health. But what was on the inside impressed me more. Kind and conscientious, he was one of the most loyal people I have ever met. These were also traits that Kelly valued, and through their mutual respect and incredible adventures, the two of them established a bond that no one could break.

Brian quickly became part of our family, and the kids and I fell in love with him. He and Kelly were so funny together. We sat around the dinner table and laughed at their stories until we couldn't breathe anymore. It wasn't long before Brian learned that being part of the family also meant that as Kelly's partner in crime, he could get in as much trouble as Kelly did.

One day, Kelly and Brian came up with the great idea of putting an ice-climbing wall on the side of our two-story wood house. I had just arrived home when Jack, age ten at the time, ran out to tell me what Dad was planning.

"Oh, really," I said.

As I walked into Kelly's office and confronted him, he looked at Jack and said, "You snitch." Jack looked confused. He could not understand why I did not also love the idea.

Kelly explained that he and Brian had found this really cool foam material that they could apply to the outside of the house and then swing their ice axes and climb up the side.

I promptly replied, "You've got to be kidding. You guys will go up once and get bored. Then every child on the block will come over and throw sharp objects into the side of our house. The answer is no."

Kelly puffed up and said, "We're doing it."

Upon seeing his reaction, I knew I had only one option, and that was to play the Lou Ann card. There was only one person who could talk immediate sense into Kelly when he had his mind made up, and that was my mother-in-law.

I told him, "All right. If you are going to be that way, I'm going to call your momma."

Kelly quickly became concerned and blurted out, "Don't you call my momma."

I dialed the phone and explained the situation to Lou Ann.

Lou Ann said only three words: "Put him on."

Within one minute I heard Kelly say, "I am being sweet, Mom. I promise. I am being sweet."

Needless to say, we never got the ice wall, and Brian followed up with a bunch of flowers. To this day, Lou Ann and I laugh about that ice-climbing wall and Kelly's and Brian's rapid change of heart when Momma Lou Ann said, "No."

TO AN OUTSIDER, ADVENTURE AND ROMANCE MAY HAVE APPEARED TO BE our main attractions. But the greatest bond Kelly and I shared was our faith. When we met, I thought I knew what faith was all about, but I noticed there was something very different about Kelly. He possessed a deep sense of excitement and optimism about life and death that I did not have. As I watched and listened to him, I quietly thought, *What does he know or have that I don't?* I was eager to learn, and he thrived on helping me understand more about real faith. Throughout our relationship, he encouraged and directed me. Many nights, we sat in our living room in front of the fire and talked about our purpose in this life.

As a couple, we made a pact that we would keep our eyes on God instead of each other. Our theory was that being human, we were bound to disappoint each other. If we looked to God as the answer, everything else would fall into place. As we grew spiritually, it was as if our souls were cemented together. I never ceased to be amazed at the amount of happiness, adventure, and love my husband brought into my life. For that I will be eternally grateful.

FOUR

A Charmed Year

FOR KELLY AND ME, 2006 WAS A MAGICAL YEAR. KELLY'S CAREER AS A landscape architect was soaring. At age forty-eight his incredible talent and expertise in modern design were capturing national attention. His projects had been published in *Metropolitan Home* and *Better Homes and Gardens,* along with several design magazines and Dallas area publications. Kelly had a wonderful office at our home, and when he designed something sensational,

Colleen Duffley Photography

Kelly's pool design appeared in *Metropolitan Home* in October 2005.

I could hear his excitement throughout the house. His passion for good design inspired me, and I loved to watch the joy on his face as he meticulously explained every detail in his drawings to me.

But Kelly's excitement wasn't contained to what he did. He was just as enthusiastic about everything I did. In 2001, I started painting when he and

Brian were on one of their climbing trips. Climbing and adventure were the only reasons that Kelly and I were ever apart. One weekend, I decided that I needed a hobby too. With no prior art training, I painted a copy of a very expensive painting we saw in Santa Fe, New Mexico. To my shock, I perfectly duplicated the painting in the art brochure we had kept as a souvenir from the gallery, knowing we could never afford the original.

When Kelly arrived home, I told him I had a surprise and showed him my painting. At first, he thought I had purchased the painting. I explained what I had done and told him the grand cost of $58.27. He shook his head, laughed, and dropped all his climbing gear in the living room. Then he ran to the garage to get the hammer and nails to hang my painting on the wall. That became a tradition we would repeat climbing trip after climbing trip. After he got home and unloaded his gear, we stayed up late into the night talking about my new piece of art and his journey to the summit. It was a time we treasured.

Kelly and me at my first art gallery exhibit in 2006.

With Kelly's encouragement, I started painting original works, and in the summer of 2006 I had my first gallery showing. The night of the opening, my heart swelled as I heard him continuously brag on me and identify himself by saying, "I'm *her* husband."

Kelly was also instrumental in pushing me to make a life change and leave my vice president position at a large public relations agency to gain a better life balance. I wanted to spend more time with Kelly and with my mother, who had fallen ill.

One Saturday over coffee, I asked Kelly, "What do you think about Jessica and me going into business together?" He jumped out of his seat and said, "Are you kidding? You and Jessica are a dynamic duo together." Jessica Nuñez was a former colleague of mine and a good friend whom I greatly admired and respected.

Over the next couple of months, Kelly had boundless encouragement for me. After more than twenty years in communications as a reporter and a public relations consultant, I was ready to step out on my own. In the fall of 2006, Jessica and I formed a boutique public relations agency. When the company officially launched, Kelly smiled and said, "You now get to have your own company Christmas party. I can't wait to come and sit next to one of the owners."

No matter what was happening in my life, I always knew Kelly would be my greatest fan, and I was his. To the surprise of both of us, we weren't the only ones who appeared interested in our story. A *Dallas Morning News* reporter became aware of Kelly's incredible designs, my art, and our home renovation and asked if he could do a story. We were extremely flattered and immediately said yes. The story was called "Remodel Relationship, For Better, Worse, or Remodeling." It described how we took on the "ultimate marital challenge: a live-in whole-house renovation." What appealed to the reporter was that we had rolled up our sleeves and done most of the work ourselves. With Kelly's design capabilities and carpentry skills and my drywall and painting ability, we had dramatically renovated our home on a limited budget.

The day the article was to be published I tumbled out of bed at 5:00 a.m. and raced to the convenience store. With a stack of papers in hand, I ran into the house, turned on all the bedroom lights, and jumped on the bed, telling Kelly to wake up.

As we read the article, we giggled like little kids. We looked at each other and then sealed the moment with a kiss. We knew we had something very special, and to see a glimpse of it in print was a memory for a lifetime. Kelly and I were living a charmed life and enjoying every minute of it.

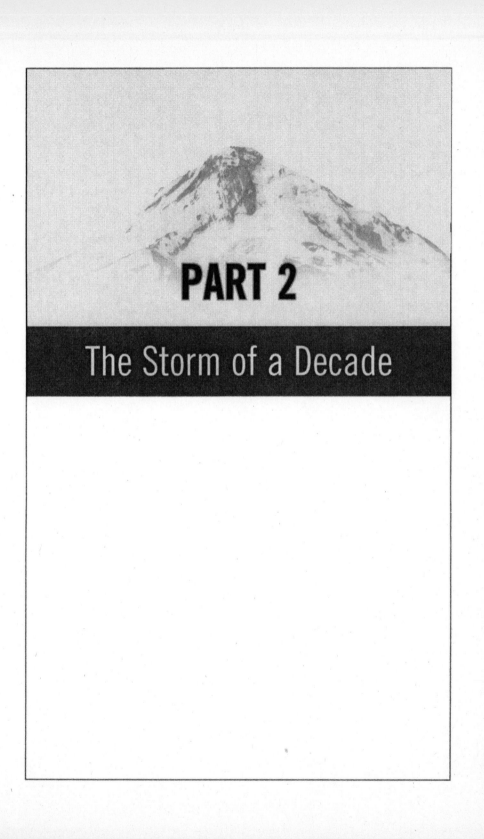

PART 2

The Storm of a Decade

FIVE

The Phone Call
That Changed My Life

WITH A WHIRLWIND SUCCESSFUL YEAR BEHIND US, KELLY AND I WERE looking forward to the holidays. He was going on a quick weekend climbing trip, and then we planned to slow down and enjoy Christmas. Kelly had been looking forward to his December trip to Mount Hood since he and Brian met another climber named Jerry "Nikko" Cooke while climbing Mount Rainier. That summer of 2006, Kelly and Brian had chosen to climb a new and more technical route called Liberty Ridge. Along the way to the summit, they climbed awhile with Nikko, a lawyer from New York, and his climbing partner, Willy Nash. They all hit it off immediately and admired each other's climbing skills. At one point, they said good-bye so Kelly and Brian could forge ahead.

Associated Press

Michaela and Jerry "Nikko" Cooke at their engagement.

When Kelly left the mountain, he called me and spoke about his new-found friends. He made friends faster than anyone I knew, and he was an excellent friend, always available to talk, help out, and give advice. During our conversation, he said that he was starting to get worried about his new friends because he had not seen them come down off the mountain yet. Kelly and Nikko had exchanged phone numbers, and on his flight layover in Denver, Kelly decided to call Nikko's wife, Michaela, introduce himself, and make sure that Nikko had made it down safely. She told Kelly that she had heard from Nikko and that he was fine. Michaela and I would later reflect on their new friendship and Kelly's call of concern, never anticipating that she and I would become bonded in a way we never could have imagined.

Wednesday, December 6

Kelly got up early, gathered his climbing gear together, and kissed me good-bye. He said, "Pray for me on Friday. It will be my toughest day."

We embraced and said, "I love you."

I looked at him and said seriously, "Don't you leave me." I was referring to a statement I had repeated many times before when we had our heart-to-heart discussions about his climbing and its effects on me. It scared me; I didn't know how I could go on if anything happened to him. Since his proposal, my outdoor excursions were reserved for rock climbing on family camping trips, and I was more comfortable staying at home than venturing up thousands of feet on an icy mountain. In addition, Kelly was a serious climber who scaled mountains way beyond my athletic abilities.

Kelly smiled, looked me deep in the eyes, and said, "I will never leave you."

I quickly responded, "Promise?"

"I promise," he replied.

With that, he was out the door and off to pick up Brian to catch their flight. Like clockwork, Kelly called that night, and he talked about the upcoming climb and the excitement that he and the guys shared.

Once again, he asked me to pray for him on Friday. I said I would, and he said, "I'll call you as soon as I get off the mountain. I love you very much."

Thursday, December 7

I didn't expect a call from Kelly on Thursday because he probably would not have cell phone coverage. With time on my hands, I decided to decorate the Christmas tree. Kelly, Jack, and I had picked out our tree a few days before he left but had not had a chance to decorate it. As a landscape architect and outdoors enthusiast, Kelly was a stickler for real trees and would spend the month of December walking through our living room saying, "Smell that pine! Love it!" During our marriage, I had never decorated the tree without Kelly. But I was concerned that by the time he got home and we found time together to work on the tree, it would almost be Christmas. Kelly had not taken a trip in December before, so this year I decided to surprise him with it all lit up. Over the years Kelly had grown to appreciate and have fun with the wild Christmas trees I planned. He knew that this year we were having a modern orange and hot pink tree, and he would just laugh at my childlike excitement of getting to decorate it.

As I went out to the garage to get the decorations, the thought occurred to me, *Am I jinxing things?* I immediately put the thought out of my mind: *No, you don't believe in things like that. God's in control . . . so stop that kind of thinking.*

Sunday, December 10, Before Noon

Because of the upcoming holiday and my busy schedule trying to set up our new business, I opted not to paint while Kelly was away this time. It was a beautiful Sunday, so I decided to help my mom plant bulbs in her garden. Kelly would be home on Monday, and I thought it would be good to spend time with Mom. Although divorced, both my parents, Ann and Roy Oddy, still lived in Dallas, in addition to my younger brother, Karl, and we all remained very close as a family. My mother had developed cardiomyopathy and had undergone a couple of heart surgeries. Spending time with her now was a top priority in my life. Shortly before noon, I decided to take a break from the garden and check my voice mail.

It was the call I feared most, and it was the introduction to the worst nightmare of my life. The voice on the other end explained that Kelly, Brian, and their friend Nikko Cooke had missed their pickup time at the base of Mount Hood. The man's voice said the sheriff wanted to make sure that I had not heard from Kelly before they launched a search party.

I told my mother about the call. She hugged me and said, "Go!" Just as I started out the front door, she stopped me: "Wait, you forgot these," and handed me a bag full of bulbs to plant in my garden.

As I drove home, my first call was to Ford, Kelly's twenty-three-year-old son. "Meet me at the house," I said. "Dad is missing, and I need you to help me go through his e-mail and climbing plans to give the sheriff all the details we can find."

The fifteen-minute drive seemed to take an eternity. The whole time I prayed again and again: "Please, God, not now. We still have so much to do together."

Soon Ford raced into the house and asked, "What's happened?"

After I explained the situation, we went into Kelly's office to go through his computer files. Ford had been working with his dad, and I knew that they had talked about the trip. By piecing together what Kelly had told me, his conversations with Ford, and his e-mail correspondence with Brian and Nikko, I was hoping to provide the sheriff with as much valuable information as possible.

I had not talked to Kelly since Wednesday night, but he had warned me that cell phone reception might be spotty on the mountain. I was not to worry if I did not hear from him during the next few days. Despite Kelly's comment, the kids and I had been calling him throughout the weekend, which was pretty typical of us while he was away. We independently called to see, just by chance, if he had cell phone reception. So far, no one had been able to reach him.

Sheriff Joseph Wampler of Hood River, Oregon, was in charge of investigating the report of the missing climbers. I dialed the number that was left on my voice mail, and within minutes into our conversation, I knew he was taking this missing climbers' report very seriously. I explained that Kelly had more than twenty-five years of climbing experience. Then I relayed all I knew about Kelly's plans, which he had described to me the night before he left.

Kelly, Brian, and Nikko planned to spend two nights on the mountain. They would start at the parking lot of Cooper Spur Lodge, climb the north face, summit, and then go down the south side and end up at Timberline Lodge. A friend of Brian's would pick them up at Timberline and drive them to their rental car parked near the north side of the mountain. They were not going to come down the north side, the route they climbed up, because of the technical difficulty of down climbing it. They were to spend

Associated Press

Sheriff Joseph Wampler directing the search and rescue.

both nights on the mountain, but Kelly mentioned that they were going to check out an old cabin, which I later learned was called Tilly Jane.

According to Kelly's e-mail, they were looking forward to going to the lodge on Saturday afternoon, after getting off the mountain, for a well-deserved round of beer. Nikko was scheduled to fly out early Sunday morning, and Kelly and Brian would spend an extra day to take advantage of some snowboarding before they returned home on Monday, December 11.

The sheriff listened intently and informed me that the weather was getting bad, but they were going to send a snowcat, a vehicle designed to move on snow, up to Tilly Jane before it got dark. He would call us back at 8:00 p.m.

Search and rescue team loading a snowcat.

Sunday, December 10, Afternoon

The family needed to be together at the house to hear the sheriff's report. I called Jason, age twenty-five, and Katie, age twenty, and asked them to come over but not to call and worry Jack, age twelve. Jack was over at his mom's house, and I saw no reason to upset him at this point.

As a former journalist, I had spent more than ten years as a TV news reporter at ABC, NBC, and CBS affiliates across the country, working the majority of the time with law enforcement on the crime beat. My past experience told me that the sheriff's tone and explanation of the terrain made clear that it was a serious situation. While we were waiting for Jason and Katie, I called Kelly's dear friend and former climbing partner, Keith Airington.

"Keith, something's not right. Kelly is missing on Mount Hood. I'm talking with the sheriff, but I'm scared and not sure what to do."

He responded exactly as I knew he would: "Hold on, girl. He's tough, and I'm sure he's okay. I'll make some calls right now. Call me immediately if you hear anything. Hang in there."

Keith had taught Kelly how to climb in college, and the two had remained incredibly close throughout the years. Kelly reflected his admiration for his friend by giving Jack the middle name of Airington. Before long, Keith called back and said, "Hey, I have been on the phone with Steve Rollins, the rescue leader of Portland Mountain Rescue. Here's his number if you want to call him. I'm going to make some more calls. Don't worry. We'll find him!"

Despite Keith's reassurance, something in my gut told me this was the real deal and the greatest fear of being a climber's wife.

Kelly with his first climbing partner, Keith Airington.

Sunday, December 10, Early Evening

Jason was the first to arrive, and he joined Ford and me in my office upstairs. Immediately Ford and I started to update Jason. After we explained the situation, the room fell quiet. Each of us was searching for the answer of what to do next. I started praying for the phone to ring.

Then Jason asked, "Has anyone tried to call Dad?"

Ford and I replied together, "Yes!" We had tried dozens of times, but our calls kept rolling over to voice mail.

Jason pulled out his cell phone. "I'm going to try," he said and dialed

Kelly's number. He got a puzzled look on his face and said, "It's ringing." But the call eventually went to voice mail, so he hung up.

A couple of seconds later, Jason's phone rang. I nervously wondered, *Kelly?*

Jason quickly answered it, listened, and yelled, "Dad?"

Kelly heard the phone ring and called Jason back.

Jason asked, "Dad, where are you?" By the expression on his face, we knew Kelly was in trouble.

Both of the older boys had been climbing many times with their father, and everything Kelly taught them kicked into full gear. Jason and Ford went into rapid-fire mode, asking every search and rescue question possible. Kelly responded that he was in a gully in a snow cave on the north side of Mount Hood, just below the summit.

The boys repeated this question several times to ensure that Kelly really knew where he was, and they followed it up by asking him for nearby landmarks. Ford was writing down the information for the rescue workers, who would need every possible detail to try to find him.

Their next question was, "Where are Brian and Nikko?"

Kelly responded, "Brian is in town getting help, and Nikko's on a plane." He added that he was cold, wet, and weak.

When they asked if he was hurt, Kelly said, "No."

They then followed up: "Are you okay?"

Kelly responded, "No."

The boys asked, "Dad, do you have anything to eat?"

Kelly replied, "I have half an orange."

While the boys were talking to Kelly, I called the sheriff on the house phone to let him know that we were on the line with Kelly, and I confirmed that he was in trouble and that it would be a rescue mission. I held the phone out so the sheriff could hear the one-way conversation with Kelly. The boys told their dad that we were talking to the sheriff's office and that they were launching search and rescue to come and get him.

Then it was my turn to talk with my husband. I knew the boys had gathered all the information needed for the rescue. My only focus was to sound strong and positive and give him hope while he was in that snow cave, cold and alone.

Fighting back the tears, I could hear my voice crack as I said, "Hi, honey."

With as much energy as possible, he said, "Hey, baby."

I was taken aback that he was struggling to talk. As a climber's wife, I had heard from Kelly the worst-case climbing scenarios, and I knew he was definitely in trouble. As strange as it sounds, I could sense he was bitterly cold. His voice was weak and sluggish.

My body started to react to the seriousness of the situation. I felt as if I wanted to throw up. Standing was difficult because my knees wanted to buckle under me. But I was determined to try to give him as much encouragement as possible to fight the cold and what was happening to him.

I said, "Honey, I just decorated the Christmas tree, and it's really pretty. You have to come home and see it."

I could almost hear Kelly smile as he mustered up the strength to say, "I will."

Then I said, "Kelly James, I love you so much."

And he replied with a heartfelt "I love you too."

Fearing the hypothermia would take hold and he might not wake up, I urged him to stay awake. I was later surprised to learn that the sheriff had heard my plea to Kelly over the house phone that I had laid down on the desk. He would later tell a reporter it was a "heart-jerker."

Kelly knew *I knew* he was in bad shape. But we did not acknowledge that to each other because neither of us could face that it could be our last good-bye. Before we hung up, I passed along a message from the sheriff's department to turn off his phone and conserve his cell phone battery. As my tears started to flow, I could no longer talk.

The boys took over, saying, "Dad, help is on the way. They are coming to get you. Hang in there."

When we hung up, I broke down. Kelly was in trouble; help had to reach him soon. As I sat on the sofa, crying, the boys put their arms around me, and I could feel their concern increasing.

Within a few minutes, the fighter in me kicked in. I stood up and said, "We are going to go and get him." To gain support for myself and the effort, I called my girlfriends, who responded immediately. Kathleen and my business partner, Jessica, went into full action mode, helping me decide next steps and map out travel logistics. With the physical plans in motion, my dear friend Ellen Miller went to work on the spiritual front and organized a prayer chain that night to pray for the safe return of Kelly, Brian, and Nikko. In addition to being my dear friend, Ellen and her husband, Steve, were also our backdoor neighbors, and Kelly and I often made the quick trip across the alley to spend time with them.

Me and my friends Ellen Miller (*left*) and Jessica Nuñez (*center*).

My next priority was to make arrangements to fly to Portland as soon as possible. After the rescue, Kelly would be taken to a hospital. Knowing that he would want us all to be there, I made the decision to pack up the family and head out on the next available flight.

Katie soon arrived, and now all three of the older kids were at the house. I called Jack's mom and explained the situation. She agreed that with all the phones ringing and the heavy cloud of concern at our house, it would be best for Jack to spend the night with her and I would pick him up on the way to the airport. We were very fortunate that Jack lived just down the street with his mom and stepdad. She said, "Let me put Jack on."

I mustered every bit of strength I had to disguise the tone of concern in my voice. But Jack was one smart twelve-year-old and picked up on things very quickly. "Hi, honey. Hey, Jason, Ford, and Katie are over here now. We are coming to get you super-early at 3:30 a.m. so we can all go together to

Associated Press

Steve Rollins, Portland Mountain Rescue Leader, searching for the climbers.

the airport. We just spoke with Dad, and he is stuck right now on the mountain. We want to be there as a family as soon as he gets down."

Jack asked, "Is Dad okay?"

I chose my words carefully: "Right now the rescue workers are getting ready to go up and get him. He will be happy that we are coming."

"Okay," said Jack. "I love you."

"Love you too."

I felt better because we were taking action, but this proved to be a fleeting moment of comfort.

While we were making our travel plans, the sheriff's department called back and said that they needed Kelly to turn on his phone. The cell phone company was trying to triangulate his signal to pinpoint the location. My heart sank since we had just told Kelly to turn off his cell phone.

Feeling helpless again, I urged the older kids, "Just pray and pray hard for your dad to turn his phone on."

With Steve Rollins's telephone number in my hand, I called the search and rescue leader and relayed our conversation with Kelly. Steve reassured me that he would be on the mountain the next day searching for Kelly.

"Thank you and please find him," I said as we ended the call.

Steve replied, "We'll do our very best."

Monday, December 11, 2:00 a.m.

My head was spinning. It was 2:00 a.m. before I got to bed, and in less than an hour I had to wake up the kids so that we could drive to the airport. I couldn't help replaying the phone conversation with Kelly. He said that Brian was in town getting help. That part made sense. But why did he say that Nikko was on a plane? Then I remembered my conversation that evening with Nikko's wife, Michaela. She said she was worried when Nikko did not arrive on his Sunday flight to New York. When we spoke with Kelly, he knew the date and the time, and he was operating under the assumption that both climbers had already made it down safely.

The fact that Kelly and Brian had separated was weighing heavily on me. The two men never would have left each other unless there was no option. Something must have gone terribly wrong.

Kelly had different responses to the boys' questions about whether he was hurt. Maybe at first he was trying not to worry us and then he reconsidered his answer. He was aware that I was with the boys during the call, and he would have wanted to protect me from knowing that he was injured. He knew it would tear me apart—and he was right. I could just imagine him thinking, *I'll explain to Karen and the kids when I get off the mountain.*

As I drifted off to sleep, I was still crying and thinking about his cell phone being turned off. The last thing I remember was saying aloud, "Honey, please, please turn on your phone. God, please make him turn on his phone."

SIX

Our Arrival

Monday, December 11, 3:00 a.m.

When the alarm rang at 3:00 a.m., it took me a few seconds to realize that the events of last night had really happened and I was not having a nightmare. Reality soon returned: my husband was trapped on Mount Hood. I reached for the phone by the side of our bed and called his cell phone. It went straight to voice mail. *He hasn't turned it back on.*

Going from bedroom to bedroom, I woke up Katie and Ford. I did not have to go back several times; they got right out of bed. It was a stark contrast to our typical early morning wake-up calls when Kelly jumped on top of them and teased them unmercifully until they finally got out of bed to get ready for a trip. This time, there were no laughs or pillow fights, just painful silence as we all mechanically loaded the suitcases in the car, knowing that the man we all loved and depended on was out of our reach and in more trouble than he had ever faced in his life. Soon Jason arrived. He too lived nearby with his wife, Sara, in a little house that Kelly had renovated for them.

We picked up Jack and quietly drove to the airport. No one was in the

51

mood to talk much. I told the kids, "Guys, keep trying to call your dad." One by one, they took turns dialing to see if he had turned on his cell phone. No luck. While we were sitting in the airport, waiting to board our flight, I tried Kelly's phone again. It was around 6:30 a.m. central time. The phone rang before rolling over to voice mail.

"Something's happened. His phone just rang," I told the kids.

Everyone gathered around, and I called the sheriff's department: "I think Kelly's turned on his phone."

The female voice at the other end said, "Let me look. We are getting monitoring reports from his cell phone provider. They are pinging him every five minutes, looking for activity to get a satellite position reading." She came back on the line and said, "No, it doesn't look like there has been any activity."

I said, "No, I know something has changed."

At that, she said, "Let me look again." There was a brief pause. "Yes, I can now see something. It looks like we got a ping around 4:20 a.m. Pacific time. Let me make a call."

As I hung up, I told the kids, "We think he just turned on his phone."

They all let out a sigh of relief, said a positive, "Yes!" and did a few high fives.

That was a great sign. It meant Kelly was still alive and had the presence of mind to save his battery and turn on his phone when rescue workers would start looking for him again. I proudly thought, *That's my guy!*

Having the reassurance that he had made it through the night was all I needed to lift my spirits. The only thing I could think of was getting my husband off that mountain alive.

As we started to board the plane, Jack said to me, "I bet Dad's in a lot of trouble when he gets home."

I had to laugh and then responded, "You better believe it. After I finish kissing him, I'm going to whoop his behind."

At that Jack grinned. Katie overheard our conversation and said in a very adult parental tone, "That's right. I'm not going to let him go anywhere again!"

The kids and I had a mission, and we were determined to get that man back to Dallas. But we were not alone. Kathleen and Jessica expanded the efforts they initiated the night before and were up early finding resources to support me and the kids in Oregon. One resource kindly came from a former colleague of mine who had recently moved to Portland and was eager to help by greeting us at the airport and driving us to Mount Hood.

Monday, December 11, 10:00 a.m.

Before we got off the plane, I told the kids that we had to stick together like glue. Everyone agreed, and Jason, Ford, and Katie looked at Jack protectively. The older kids adored Jack, and he worshiped them. There had always been six of us, but now it was five. The world was not right.

We were the last ones to leave the plane, and as we walked through the airport, I saw a man holding a sign with my name on it. Instinctively I started toward him, with the kids behind me. My former colleague, Aili Jokela, appeared from nowhere and took me by the arm. She said, "That's a reporter. Let's walk this way."

Suddenly it struck me; the tables were turned. As a former reporter, I would experience what it was like to be part of a story instead of covering it. My husband, Brian, and Nikko were the news story, and we were the distressed family. It all seemed surreal.

Leaving the airport, Aili informed us that we were going to the sheriff's office in Hood River instead of the mountain. The Emergency Operations Center (EOC) was located in the sheriff's office, and it was the command post where we would get the best information. She added that the media were at Cooper Spur Lodge, located on the north side of Mount Hood, and by going to his office, we would also avoid the cameras.

I was eager to meet Sheriff Joseph Wampler. I had talked to him on the phone and already knew he was a man of action. During my reporting days,

I gained a deep affection and appreciation for law enforcement and quickly grasped that this sheriff knew the mountain and the best way to conduct a rescue operation.

At the sheriff's office we were greeted as if we were part of the family. They welcomed us and made us feel right at home. They asked if we had a place to stay, and when I responded, "No," they booked rooms for us at a local bed-and-breakfast. They were well aware that we would not be leaving that night with Kelly.

Meeting Sheriff Wampler in person confirmed what I thought when I spoke with him on the telephone. This was definitely not his first rodeo; he was a pro at handling distressed family members. He smiled when he talked, and he was very deliberate in the words he chose.

The sheriff introduced us to Chief Deputy Jerry Brown, Detective Sergeant Gerry Tiffany, 911 Director Marita Haddan, and other impressive members of his staff. In addition, we met Captain Chris Bernard with the Air Force Reserve's 304th Rescue Squadron. As I met these remarkable people, I breathed a sigh of relief because these folks deeply cared about getting our guys off the mountain and back home safely with their families. It was this sense of caring and friendship throughout the entire ordeal that I will remember for the rest of my life.

We received updates on the rescue mission and learned more about the mountain that had enticed our loved ones away from the comfort of their homes onto its icy white peaks. At 11,239 feet, Mount Hood is the highest point in Oregon, and each year, nearly ten thousand people attempt to climb it. Most climbers choose the route on the south side of the mountain near Timberline Lodge and make the climb in the spring and summer. Kelly, Brian, and Nikko wanted to tackle some serious ice climbing, and that's why they chose to venture up the treacherous north face, above Eliot Glacier, near Cooper Spur, in the winter.

Searchers had found a note on Sunday when they were alerted that the three climbers were missing. The note, written on a piece of brown paper left on the dashboard of their rented Suburban, was dated Thursday, December 7. It read:

> *We are a party of three attempting the north face. Ranger station was closed so we couldn't buy a parking permit. We plan to sleep 12/7 on route and descend south side on Friday. We will retrieve truck Saturday afternoon. (35 will be open.) DO NOT TOW! In emergency storm we will descend Cooper Spur and have food and fuel in truck. We will be happy to pay for permit Saturday.*
>
> *Thanks, Jerry Cooke.*

Hearing about the note boosted my confidence that they were doing all the right things and would soon be found. *They are leaving a trail of their plans. That's a good thing,* I told myself.

Monday, December 11, Noon

After we had been in the EOC a couple of hours, the sheriff asked everyone to gather round. He was getting reports that searchers ascending the mountain were facing whiteout conditions. One group was able to reach 8,500 feet, but that was as high as the guys could climb.

The sheriff said, "It's a blizzard up there, and wind gusts at the summit are forecasted at ninety miles per hour and near sixty miles per hour around seven thousand feet. I'm sorry to tell you, but we've ordered a 2:00 p.m. turnaround due to the extreme weather conditions. We've got rescuers being blown off their feet, and we are worried about their safety."

Todd Wells/Crag Rats

Rescue workers hunting for the climbers in a blizzard.

My stomach sank as I recalled how weak Kelly sounded on Sunday. They needed to get him off that mountain *today*. But that was not going to happen.

He's okay. He's safe in a snow cave, I reassured myself. Snow caves provide great protection and get above freezing inside. Kelly had studied their structure, and he had dug many snow caves in the past. A good snow cave is dug slightly uphill into a snow bank and is just big enough to house the climbers so they can benefit from each other's body heat. He packed his red snow shovel for this trip, telling me that they planned to spend the night in such a shelter.

Yet I could not overcome my disappointment. We had flown all the way from Dallas, and I was prepared to swoop in, see that my husband was safe and healthy, and fly back as soon as possible with him. At this point I was in action mode and not even considering that he might have to recuperate.

I called Jessica and Kathleen to tell them that rescuers could not reach Kelly that day. In turn, they informed me that the Dallas media had already heard reports that some residents were missing on Mount Hood. I knew the rumors would only add to speculation and potential misinformation, so I agreed to release Kelly's name and explain the situation.

Soon Kathleen and Jessica called back and said they felt too close to this story because of their relationship with me and Kelly. Both were concerned that they were too emotional to serve as media spokespersons. We agreed that an old colleague, Mike Androvett, who was a former NBC reporter in Dallas turned legal consultant, would deliver the news. With a spokesperson in place, Jessica and Kathleen went to work setting up the news conference.

Shortly before the news conference in Dallas, Mike called me and asked, "Karen, is there anything you want me to say?"

"You know me and you know Kelly," I replied. "Just give it to them straight and make sure they know he's not some amateur who decided to do something stupid and beyond his ability. I trust you. Just do my man right." I paused and thought how lucky I was to have such friends. "Thank you very much."

Mike said, "Got it. Take care. We're praying for him."

As the news quickly spread in Dallas, so did the prayers. While people often joke that there is a church on every corner, the city has a strong base of residents who do not shy away from talking about their faith and showing what real faith looks like. One of these people is my dear friend Ellen, who was networking to get more people praying and obtain needed divine intervention.

The power of e-mail became apparent as the prayer requests left the churches and became mainstream in major corporations where employees forwarded the news of the climbers and the request for prayers to their colleagues. This movement spread across the country and extended to countries across the world.

The news was out, and with our arrival, the rescue mission was intensifying. However, at that point we were naïve about what would transpire. We were still under the impression that the situation would be resolved soon. Kelly would be airlifted to safety, and Brian and Nikko would be located farther down the mountain, seeking shelter from the storm. Never in our wildest nightmare did we dream that our first night in Oregon would be one of many as our loved ones lay on a snowy battlefield in a fierce war between man and nature.

SEVEN

An Unbelievable Response

GETTING THE FAMILY TO MOUNT HOOD HAD KEPT ME FOCUSED ON MOVING forward, but now sitting quietly in the EOC, I was forced to digest the severity of the situation. As I thought about next steps, Jessica called and said that Kelly's oldest brother, Frank James, was on his way. Frank was flying in from his home in Orlando, Florida, and was to meet me at the sheriff's department.

Throughout the years, I have had the pleasure to become close to Frank and his wife, Carolyn, as they have stayed with us during their visits to Dallas. He would bring the stability we all needed.

I was also eager to have Frank in Mount Hood because we needed him for much more than moral support. Shortly before Frank arrived, I had another conversation with Jessica and Kathleen. They said, "Karen, you need to have a family spokesperson up there with you. You have always talked about how great Kelly's older brother, Frank, is. What about him?"

"Excellent idea," I replied. "I'll ask him." I was so grateful that Jessica and Kathleen were helping us think through things. They enabled me to concentrate on Kelly, the kids, and the rescue mission.

When Frank walked into the EOC, I gave him a big hug. We looked into each other's eyes, clearly understanding that his little brother and my husband was in a very bad situation. Before Frank joined the other family members, I spoke to him privately and briefed him on everything I could think of. Frank listened intently. Both of us were in action mode. We were in a crisis, and neither one of us had time to give in to our emotions. We reviewed the situation and plan of attack as if we were going into war. We were in the fight of our lives to save Kelly, and we were ready for battle.

In addition to Frank, members of the climbers' families came to Hood River. Lou Ann, Kelly's mom; Traci Hale, his youngest sister; and Jason's wife, Sara, flew in to stay with us at the bed-and-breakfast. Brian's sister, Angela Hall, and his parents, Clara and Dwight Hall, arrived. It was good to see Clara and Dwight again—just not in those circumstances. Kelly and I had met them a couple of years ago when Brian brought them over to our house for dinner. Nikko's wife, Michaela, and her best friend, along with Nikko's mom, Maria Kim, made the trip. But the support did not stop with immediate family. Dozens of friends and loved ones showed up to offer their assistance.

Due to the growing size of the group, the sheriff relocated us to a conference room adjacent to the EOC. Despite our numbers, the sheriff and his staff, along with Captain Bernard, always made time to answer questions and speak with every concerned family member.

There was definitely no shortage of emotional resources.

Tuesday, December 12, 10:00 a.m.

The day began with great excitement. We had news that rescuers started out early at 6:00 a.m. and that the Army National Guard had launched a Black Hawk helicopter around 9:00 a.m. to aid in the search.

We also got a sense of the strong commitment to find the climbers and the multiple organizations involved. In addition to the Hood River County Sheriff's Office, the Air Force Reserve's 304th Rescue Squadron, and National Guard, we learned about the participation of the Clackamas County Sheriff's Office, Portland Mountain Rescue, Corvallis Mountain

Rescue, and a volunteer rescue group called the Crag Rats. The oldest mountain search and rescue organization in the United States, the Crag Rats regularly participated in Mount Hood rescues. The Hood River County Sheriff's Office commanded the north face search teams, and the Clackamas County Sheriff's Office oversaw the search teams on the south face. Searchers also received assistance from Mountain Waves, a group of outdoor enthusiasts with a deep background in technology and communications, who were part of the team that helped identify the signal of Kelly's cell phone.

Teams and equipment traveled an hour's ride more than ten miles up a steep, unplowed road to Cloud Cap Inn, which was functioning as the base camp and was located at about six thousand feet. Some searchers spent the night at the inn to get an early morning start.

Associated Press

Rescuers gather at the Cloud Cap Inn following their search of Mount Hood.

Boosted by news of the resources and the day's forecast of calmer weather, our confidence soon dropped. Half a foot of snow fell on the mountain overnight, and additional snowfall was predicted. Despite an early morning search, there was still no word on the missing climbers.

Tuesday, December 12, Early Afternoon

The families' first news conference on the mountain was held that afternoon. I gathered the families together and explained, "Frank is going to be our family spokesperson, and we want to review with everyone what he is going to say to ensure that everyone is comfortable." I added, "Anyone can speak. But if you would like for Frank to say a few words on behalf of everyone, he will be happy to do so."

Earlier when I talked to Frank about taking on this job, he accepted his role, knowing what had to be done. As Frank addressed the families, they immediately connected with him. They could tell that his concern was for more than his brother. He was truly worried about all three men, and he was prepared to help in any way that he could. It was unanimous among the other families to have Frank represent all three climbers' families before the news media.

As Frank was gathering his things to leave for the news conference, I asked, "Do you have a jacket?"

He pointed to the lightweight coat he was wearing. I shook my head and said, "You need more than that."

I had brought an extra suitcase for Kelly and packed his orange down jacket. He had opted to take his heavier blue jacket on this trip, but I thought he would probably need a clean jacket once he came off the mountain. I offered it to Frank: "Take Kelly's orange jacket. It's sure to bring both you and Kelly luck. As you can see, I'm wearing the matching jacket."

Frank laughed and said, "You and Kelly have matching jackets?" Frank knew Kelly as well as I did, and the thought of him having matching clothing with his wife was way out of character.

"Yes," I said with a smile. "He was wearing it when he proposed, so I call it his engagement jacket. He will want it when he comes down, so take good care of it."

He looked at me and said, "I will, Sister."

No one anticipated the media whirlwind that was about to break loose. Frank introduced himself on behalf of all the families, and he addressed the reporters gathered outside in the cold: "Today we are keeping big hope alive for our missing family members."

He provided additional details of the events from the families' perspective. Then the news conference took a turn with statements that are often edited out of the evening news. Being a man of faith, Frank understood that none of the families or the guys could survive this ordeal without God's help. He knew that both Kelly and Brian were Christians, and once on the ground in Hood River he talked with Nikko's family and friends to learn more about him and what he believed.

He went on to say, "Today is a day for courage and for prayers. Courage can help us see our way through this snowstorm. And prayers can move mountains."

All three men were believers, and Frank thought that in addition to the facts and weather reports, it was important to reveal the character of the men trapped on the mountain. He explained to the media that all three of the men "are men of faith." For the families, this statement was just a fact, but we would start to see a reaction that was completely unexpected as others wanted to learn much more about the men who were capable of embracing both an extreme sport and God.

Watching Frank in action, I was so proud of him, and I knew Kelly would be too. I couldn't wait for Kelly to get down off the mountain and banter back and forth with Frank. Kelly would tease Frank in a way that only a brother can. Some of my fondest memories of Kelly and Frank were at our home when the refined theologian reverted to a competitive, playful adolescent as he and Kelly lovingly picked on each other and attempted to outwit each other.

Tuesday, December 12, Late Afternoon

Back at the EOC, Sheriff Wampler and Captain Bernard gathered the families for a briefing. Disappointment set in when the sheriff told us that the helicopter could not get above six thousand feet because of the powerful winds. Although it couldn't get high enough to look for the snow cave, almost forty searchers had spent the day on lower areas of the mountain in case Brian and Nikko had gotten lost as they descended the mountain's fall line, a common mistake of missing climbers. The sheriff added, "Some of the crews got to around seventy-two hundred feet while others made it to nine thousand."

But the sheriff did not want us to leave totally discouraged and updated us on activity surrounding Kelly's cell phone. They had made progress pinpointing his phone. Two points were found with a very high probability of accuracy. The signals came from about eleven thousand feet on Mount Hood and were close to the summit. The signals also suggested that the phone was moved from one point to another and that the points were not far from each other.

Authorities noted that by triangulating his phone, they could come within about 1,640 feet of his actual location. He said, "We are text messaging him, but he has not responded."

I rationalized to myself, *Well, Kelly doesn't really use text messaging. Maybe he just didn't see it.*

Although 1,640 feet seemed to be a large search area, I took comfort that it was in the exact location that Kelly had described on the phone. I was relieved to have additional confirmation that Kelly was not in a state of confusion when we spoke to him on his cell phone and that he knew exactly where he was and what was going on.

Despite this positive news, I was very much aware that the days were passing by, and the guys still were on the mountain. We inquired, "What about tomorrow?" Up to four feet of snow were expected to blanket the mountain over the next couple of days. The avalanche danger was extremely high. The sheriff said, "Folks, I have got to tell you it doesn't look good for the search tomorrow, but we will be here on standby, ready to go as soon as we get a break in the weather."

As I left the EOC on Tuesday night, I had no idea about how much attention this story was getting nationally and how many resources of people and materials would arrive on Wednesday and contribute to the effort to get these guys off this mountain.

Wednesday, December 13, 8:00 a.m.

As Wednesday arrived, so did the resources. At the EOC, the sheriff was excited to brief us that reinforcements were on their way. The heavy media attention was sparking interest from climbers across the country, eager to volunteer for this search and rescue mission. In addition to new rescue workers, the ones who had been tirelessly searching day after day were refusing to give up. We were told that representatives from a Colorado company called Alliance for Robot-Assisted Crisis Assessment and Recovery, or ARACAR, were driving in and donating the services of five of their planes equipped with heat-sensing cameras to search for the climbers. Each of these unmanned

Associated Press

Mike Iwanick from the Alliance for Robot-Assisted Crisis Assessment and Recovery (ARACAR) displays a drone, a heat-sensitive, unmanned aircraft that was used in the search.

computer-controlled planes, called drones, was about eighteen inches long with a battery-powered motor. The rescue workers were hoping the planes could go into areas that were too dangerous to climb.

I was also shocked to hear that the FBI was on its way to work with a defense contractor who was providing private phone-tracking technology to help pinpoint Kelly's location using his cell phone. Kelly's cell phone company had narrowed down the area, but this defense company had the technology to narrow the search area even further.

Many people cared enough to take time out and donate resources to try to help in the rescue. From corporate America donating its precious technology to the kind residents who brought by a DVD player and movies to keep Jack occupied, the incredible outpouring overwhelmed us. For some reason, the story had captured the nation's attention, prayers, and strong desire to help these three men survive. Sheriff Wampler summed it up: "I've never seen anything like this!"

Though disconnected from the outside world, I heard about another response to the story too. Friends told me that others were criticizing the guys and complaining about the resources being used to try to save their lives. I was not angry at the criticism, but I was sad that they had not had the pleasure of meeting the three phenomenal men. I knew in my heart that if any one of those critics was in trouble, Kelly, Brian, and Nikko would be the first in line to help. With their kind and good natures, I was certain that when our guys were off the mountain and had time to recover, they would do something incredible for everyone who helped in the rescue.

While the families remained at the EOC during the search, we were kept aware of the activity at Cloud Cap, and we decided to let the rescue workers know how much we appreciated their efforts. All three families got into the spirit of things and came up with the idea to send food and energy drinks on the snowcat to the Cloud Cap base camp. We started by handwriting a message on a poster board and loaded up several cases of energy drinks to be transported up the mountain.

We later learned that the gift of thanks was warmly received, and the rescue workers posted our sign inside the base camp. Our message read, "Rescue Workers, you are our Rock Stars! Thank you for your energy and commitment. These are all-American boys. We are praying for your safety as you bring them home to us. Love, the families of Kelly, Brian & Jerry."

304th Rescue Squadron

The search and rescue base camp at Cloud Cap with our sign posted on the wall.

Throughout the week, we followed up with more food. It wasn't much, but we wanted the incredible rescuers to know that we never lost sight of or took for granted what they were doing for our families.

Wednesday, December 13, Afternoon

Knowing the emotional toll we must be under, once again my former employer stepped in and asked Jessica who I would want with us to deal with the media. The offer thrilled me. Frank was juggling interview after interview, and we needed help on the ground to coordinate the multiple media requests. Jessica and Kathleen had been handling them over the phone, but the intensity of the news story was heating up. I thought it was ironic that even though I dealt with the media for a living, I was unable to help Frank with the interviews in Hood River. But both he and I understood our roles, and mine was to focus on the search and the behind-the-scenes efforts.

It took me about two seconds to respond positively to the offer. I told Jessica: "That's an easy one. Do you think Ashley and Bill could come?"

Ashley Blaker and Bill Palen are two of the most incredible men I have ever met, both personally and professionally. They are extremely talented public relations professionals, but most important, they have a sense of integrity and insight not found often enough in corporate America. Kelly liked both of them very much, and they had been to our home several times. But their talent and friendship weren't the only reasons behind my request. Both men are strong believers. Anyone interacting within this tight family circle, under these circumstances, had to understand God and our faith.

When Ashley and Bill arrived, they hugged me, and I cried. I had been through so many professional situations with these two men. Their presence made me feel safe because I knew they would take care of the families. I thought, *Kelly's glad you are here.*

After they had been with us only an hour, Frank came up to me and said, "These men are amazing."

I smiled and said, "I told you so."

People who knew Kelly were prepared to go to great lengths to get him off the mountain. While I was speaking with one of the deputies he asked me, "Do you know a Doug Black in Dallas?"

I responded, "Yes, he's one of Kelly's best friends."

"Well, let me tell you that is one nice guy. He has called several times asking what he can do to help and offering any kind of financial support to get him down."

I just smiled and shook my head. I was deeply touched.

The story continued to build as the media described two other notes left by the climbers. They were responsible and conscientious climbers who wanted authorities to know who they were and what they were doing. The authorities told us, "It is unheard of to find three notes."

While the first one was left on the dashboard of their rental car, the guys also slipped a handwritten note in the mail slot of the Hood River National Forest office describing the equipment they planned to take and a brief list of the mountains they had climbed. The note read:

Hello. We are three climbers: Jerry Cooke, Brian Hall and Kelly James. Attempting the north face today, Thursday, 12-7. Hiking in with gear. Attempt north face Friday and will descend at timberline. We have food, fuel, ropes, shovel, bivy sacks, heavy parkas, etc. . . We have experience on Rainier, Denali, South American expedition, etc. . .

In the third one, they expressed their gratitude. Searchers found this note in the log book at the Tilly Jane A-frame, the same place I had described to the sheriff while on the phone with him on Sunday night. Tilly Jane was built in the 1930s to provide shelter and warmth for those in the outback. The guys had spent the night there on Thursday. The note stated:

Thanks for your hard work on this great Shelter. We did not plan on staying, but the warmth of the fire changed our minds. We climb as a group of 3 and we left a $20 bill. We will leave tomorrow for the north face! Wish us luck! Nikko, B Hall, Krazy Kelly.

Based on the signature and the fact that he would never sign it "Krazy Kelly," I knew that Kelly had not written it. But I also knew that he was instrumental in writing it. Kelly always said thanks, and a note like that was right up his alley. Actually it was in the character of all three men. They were just good guys who appreciated the things and the people around them.

The more the rescue workers learned and the more we talked, we could tell that they felt connected to our families and the guys. Captain Bernard was wonderful to us and was in constant contact. After investigators found their equipment list stashed in left-behind belongings, he commented, "I always knew they were squared away, but it just tells me they did all the right things."

Captain Chris Bernard of the Air Force Reserve's 304th Rescue Squadron holds the note left by the three climbers at the ranger station. Frank looks on.

Although the rescuers had their notes, we were still missing the guys, and Wednesday shed no new light on their location. We had been through another bad weather day, and searchers once again were limited to the tree line, facing blinding snow at higher elevations. Despite the technological advances, the unmanned drones were grounded by the weather. While I continued to be extremely grateful for all the resources, another day had gone by, and Kelly was still on the mountain, away from me and his family. As I learned Thursday's forecast, I felt lightheaded. They were predicting the worst storm of the season would hit that night with winds at more than one hundred miles per hour and dump another foot of snow on the mountain.

Please, God, let us find him on Thursday before the storm, I prayed.

Thursday, December 14, Morning

I woke up early, and before I left the room at the bed-and-breakfast, I gently awakened each of the kids. I said, "I'm going to the sheriff's department. You can keep sleeping, and I will call if anything happens. Don't worry. Today's going to be a good day." Hearing that statement, with their eyes still closed, they smiled.

The kids still believed that a successful rescue and happy ending were strong possibilities. For that I was very grateful. After all, they knew their dad, and they had all the confidence in the world in his survival ability. I could see Kelly's "can do" attitude in them. He never would have wanted us to give up looking for him or lose hope that he could make it out alive.

At the EOC, I found the usual buzz of activity. My setting out for the sheriff's department as Frank ran off to an early morning news conference had become our new way of life. Frank was to hold another news conference in twenty minutes. My phone rang, and Kathleen and Jessica told me, "Karen, you need to join Frank. People want to know more about the guys and want to hear from you."

I had mentally checked out of the media aspect of the search, so their comment caught me by surprise. "Do I really need to do this?" I asked. The gals responded, "Yes, it is important."

Friends of the family volunteered to drive me to Cooper Spur Inn where the news conference was to take place. Sitting in the backseat on our way up there, I looked out the window and thought, *What should I say?* Then something happened contrary to everything that I had ever experienced professionally. I really wasn't concerned about what to say. I could talk forever about my husband, his capabilities, and his faith.

The weather was terrible; it was bitterly cold with freezing rain. I could only imagine the horrible conditions the guys were facing above us on the mountain. I walked over to join Frank, who was gathered under a tarp with the media, waiting for the news conference to begin.

Once again Frank echoed the families' optimism. Then it was my turn to speak. I told reporters the only thing I knew for sure: "I know my husband is coming down off this mountain. He proposed to me on Mount Rainier, and we are planning our fiftieth wedding anniversary there. So I know he is coming down."

It had never dawned on me that we might never celebrate another wedding anniversary together. After all, Kelly had looked me straight in the eyes just a few days ago and promised he would never leave me.

And I believed him.

Thursday, December 14, Afternoon

Later in the day, we got exciting news that Kelly had activated his cell phone on Tuesday, December 12, at 10:55 p.m. Since the last confirmed cell phone contact was Monday morning, we were ecstatic because this new activation meant that he was conscious and able to activate his phone. Just as quickly as our hopes were raised, however, they were crushed when we learned that this report was incorrect. The last cell phone ping was actually on Tuesday at 1:51 a.m. Authorities told us that it could have been the result of a dying battery.

But the disappointing news did not stop there. The launch of the two drones did not produce any results, and once again the bad weather limited searchers to the tree line and lower.

Just when we thought the weather could not get any worse, it did. Forecasters were predicting some of the most violent weather to hit the state in the last decade. Even the media were encouraged to lock down their gear and move their satellite trucks to a more sheltered area. As Thursday came to a close, I thought I was about to lose my mind. None of this could possibly be happening. We should be getting ready to celebrate the Christmas holidays instead of waiting to find Kelly and his friends on Mount Hood. We were powerless against the harsh weather conditions. Divine intervention was the only answer.

EIGHT

Signs from Above?

AS THE SNOW AND WINDS CONTINUED TO BUILD, SO DID OUR ANXIETY. THE days were blurring together.

I came to hate 2:00 p.m. If they hadn't found the guys by then, it probably was not going to happen that day. Due to the bad weather, the rescue crews had to allow enough time to safely get down the mountain before dark.

Every day, like clockwork, Sheriff Wampler and Captain Bernard briefed us on what had happened on the mountain. We hung on their every word and just dropped our heads when they made that dreaded familiar statement: "Due to the weather, we had to call off the search early today. We are hoping to get a window tomorrow."

We were never upset with them; they were just the messengers. We always thanked them for their efforts, hugged each other, and then prayed for a better tomorrow.

After another unsuccessful day, the trip back to the bed-and-breakfast was always difficult for me. The kids were usually there before me. I had spent time as a reporter in EOC's, but the kids were more comfortable at the bed-and-breakfast where the atmosphere was not quite so tense. I was thankful they had a place to get away. Before dinner, we talked about the day's search and next steps. After dinner, everyone started to wind down.

At the bed-and-breakfast the kids and I decided to stay together in one large room with a couple of beds. Katie and I took one bed, and Jack and Ford bunked together. No one wanted to be alone. Sara and Jason stayed in a room near ours while Lou Ann and Traci stayed downstairs.

Since I am a morning person, the kids and Kelly were used to me being the first one to say good night and climb into bed. But now I hated the night.

Katie's and my bed was located under a skylight in the room, and I could hear every raindrop and gust of wind. I stared at the ceiling, looked up at the skylight, and whispered to Kelly, "Baby, we're coming for you. Please hold on."

I felt so guilty, lying in a nice warm bed, knowing he was freezing to death. "God, please don't do this," I prayed again and again. Sometimes in an effort to avoid this scene, I stayed up downstairs and just hoped I would

Me and my dad, Roy Oddy.

be too tired to keep thinking about how horrible it must be for my husband in that snow cave during blizzard conditions.

Loved ones in Dallas often called throughout the day, but I did not have the emotional strength to return their calls. In the darkness, when everyone at the bed-and-breakfast had already gone to sleep, I reached out to the people with whom I could let down my guard.

I was trying to be strong for the kids and Kelly's family, but with my mom, dad, and brother Karl I could be as weak and as scared as I really was. They all loved Kelly too and were very worried about their son-in-law and brother-in-law.

For the first time in my life I was no longer the "can do" gal ready to conquer the world. My man, my love, my protector was stuck on a mountain, and no matter what I tried to do, I just couldn't get him down. One night I called my dad and said, "Please, please, Daddy, get him down."

My dad paused, and I could hear his voice crack: "Karen, if I could, I would." He had received the father's request of a lifetime, yet he was powerless to help his daughter.

While I talked to Jessica and Kathleen throughout the day to discuss media requests and updates on the search, at night I spoke to my friend Ellen, who was my spiritual inspiration. We talked extensively about the fact that God was in control and that He had already written the ending of this story. My job now was to go through everything that was happening and keep the faith. I always ended the evenings with my calls to Ellen because when I talked about God and our faith, I gained peace and incredible strength to carry on, walk up those stairs, and face that skylight with the weather bearing down.

To say that faith kept many of the family members standing during this horrific week is an understatement.

We were unwillingly involved in something that was capturing worldwide attention. As the days progressed, so did the story. With the weather turning from bad to worse, millions of people joined in the prayers for a successful rescue. The concern for these three climbers swelled beyond our wildest dreams. I received constant reports on the many prayer services that were being held across the country. In one of them, a dear friend and member of Kelly's and my Bible study, Katherine Millet, told me about an incredible moment in one prayer service. Everyone stopped to listen to the MercyMe song "Hold Fast." Its lyrics seemed to perfectly fit the situation, and I would never again listen to this song without thinking of Kelly in that snow cave.

Frank expressed my exact thoughts in one of the news conferences. He said, "Our faith is threefold. We have faith in Kelly and Brian and Nikko; we have faith in the rescuers; and we have faith in God. And there is little doubt that our faith is being refined these days."

I had tremendous faith that our prayers were capable of moving mountains, and part of that certainty was based on the strong feeling of God's presence. I was undergoing what felt like a painful, physical, faith-changing experience in which I was just a lump of clay and God was in total control, busy molding me during a situation that had no escape, at least not for the time being.

But in all honesty, I didn't like being forced to refine my faith. For the first time, I really understood what the term *out of my control* meant. Having the love of my life stuck on a mountain and being powerless to get him down were torture.

Associated Press

Michaela Cooke and I comfort each other as rescue workers search for our husbands.

When your world falls out from underneath you and you are on your knees, there is nowhere to look but up. Suddenly everything you have claimed about your God and your faith is put to the test. During such a time, you learn where you stand with your Maker, and the most significant question of your life slaps you right in the face: Do you really believe?

The answer to this question for me is yes—I really believe. God is not a man-made concept. He is very, very real and in control of everything that happens, even the things that are beyond our comprehension.

While all of us were in great pain, I was confident that God had never left our side. He seemed to be sending us comfort through a series of events to assure us that we were not walking alone.

On Wednesday night while I was talking to a dear friend, I had the most incredible sensation of warmth rush all over my body. I had never felt anything like it before. It was so intense, I immediately thought, *God must be*

76

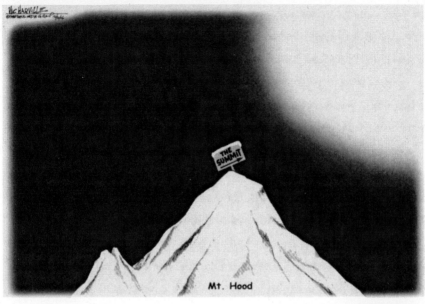

VIC HARVILLE/Stephens Media

A cartoon showing the summit and an arrow pointing to heaven ran in Kelly's mom's hometown paper, the *Benton Courier*, in Arkansas on Saturday, December 23, 2006.

telling me either everything is going to be okay or Kelly has just died. I didn't even want to consider the possibility of the latter, and I had no idea what it really meant. But this incident convinced me 100 percent that God had not abandoned me or Kelly in Oregon, and it gave me the courage to keep pushing forward throughout the week.

Another incident that seemed to defy mere coincidence involved a perfect stranger. Angela, Brian's sister, told us that one of the teenagers, now an adult, who spent thirteen days in a snow cave on Mount Hood in 1976 was offering to speak privately with the families. I was familiar with the name Randy Knapp from an article in the *Oregonian* and an interview on Larry King's show, but this survivor had remained quiet about their ordeal. Gary Schneider was now reaching out to talk with us.

The families agreed that night to meet Gary in the basement room at the Hood River Hotel. As Gary walked in, we could tell that he was not comfortable being the center of attention. He was there only because he felt compelled to do so. A friend of Gary's, who encouraged him to speak with us, explained to the group that they had come up earlier that day but were unable to locate us. Just as they were turning around to leave, they ran into a couple of Kelly's friends from Dallas, who were in Hood River to support us. Gary and his friend were very guarded in their conversation with our friends, who also provided limited information to protect the families. Eventually they revealed the purpose of the visit. The four men realized that the chance encounter was not an accident. Despite the odds, Gary and his friend had found the families by accidentally stumbling across two of Kelly's friends.

Gary described to us how he had set off with two friends on New Year's Eve in 1975 for a summit climb from Timberline Lodge on Mount Hood's south side. Just like the experience of our guys, what started as a fun, adventurous journey for three friends ended up in a fight for survival.

It's hard to convey in words what happened that night as Gary told his story and described how his faith in God protected and sustained them for thirteen days. While Gary gave God complete credit for his survival, we had renewed hope for Kelly, Brian, and Nikko. Looking back, I now realize we received more than just hope that night; God was whispering and telling us we were not alone.

Associated Press

Family and friends constantly supported each other through the long search.

The fierce storms continued, making a rescue impossible. The families stayed close together, comforting and encouraging each other. Later in the week when the weather was at its worst, the families got together for brunch. As we all sat at a long table, Frank led the prayer: "Please, Father, lift this weather and let the rescue workers reach Kelly, Brian, and Nikko." It was the same prayer we had prayed all week, but it was just as powerful as ever.

From the restaurant diners could usually view the water and the mountain. Just prior to sitting down that day, however, we could not see the mountain because of the heavy cloud cover. Shortly after our prayer, the clouds started to disappear. In amazement, we all stood up and wandered to the window. The clouds continued to lift, and for the first time we saw the mountain. Then the sun appeared, and we saw the most beautiful rainbow. It was breathtaking, and everyone started cheering. We ran out to the deck, and many in the group took pictures of the sun. I had wondered if we would ever see the sun again, and it was as if God brushed His hands across the sky and said, "Clouds begone"—and they were.

Everyone sitting at the table shook his or her head in disbelief. When the pictures of the sun were passed around on the cell phones, someone said, "It looks like the eye of God." Today those photos remain on some of the phones.

We believed that this must be a sign that a successful rescue was imminent. Then as quickly as the clouds disappeared, they returned. Once again, we were left confused and did not know what it meant, but I had no doubt that it meant something and I knew we were not alone.

Despite the harsh weather and the inability to reach the climbers throughout the week, I was still positive that our guys were coming home alive.

After all, I thought, *I do believe, and I know God is on our side.*

NINE

Give Us a Break!

Friday, December 15, Early Morning

What's that noise? I asked myself as I rolled over in bed. I could hear a strange sound but was a bit too groggy to figure it out. I was also confused about where I was. Then *boom* it hit me. Looking to my right, I could see Katie next to me, not Kelly. He was alone and cold on Mount Hood more than two miles high. *Oh, Kelly!*

The noise was rain pelting down on the skylight, and the winds were so fierce that the windows were shaking.

My heart started to race. *What time is it?* As I leaned up to look at the clock, all I could see was darkness. Feeling desperate, I asked, *Oh, God, why?*

The storms we had feared had rolled in with fury. The power was out, and what weather forecasters had been predicting had come true. The worst storm in more than a decade had just hit the Oregon coast. Ninety-mile-per-hour winds moved inland, causing flooding and knocking down trees and utility poles that left more than 350,000 Oregon homes without power. With wind gusts of up to 130 miles per hour at eleven thousand feet, the climbers were in hurricane-force winds. The effects of the storm resulted in the cancellation of ninety flights at Portland International Airport and blocked traffic along Oregon's northern coast, closing portions of most major highways.

The kids were sound asleep, and I started to cry in the darkness. *God, why are You being so tough on our family? Please, give us a break!* I begged.

As I lay warm in bed, it was more than I could bear to think that Kelly was on the mountain suffering through blizzard conditions and wind gusts in the triple digits. To believe that he was suffering while I was safe ripped me in two. I kept whispering a phrase I must have said more than one hundred times, "Baby, just hold on! Don't give up!"

Pull it together, I told myself. I had to represent our family on national TV in just a few hours. I had to snap out of this desperate attitude.

With a change in mind-set, I quietly got out of bed to keep from waking the kids. The power was still out at the bed-and-breakfast, so I called Ashley, my former colleague with us in Hood River, to talk about what we should do.

He was in the process of rounding up Michaela Cooke and Angela Hall. We decided that we would all go to the hotel where the media were staying, get ready there, and then do the early morning interviews. The power was on at that location.

The night before, Michaela, Angela, and I had decided that we would do the interviews as a team. Individually we were emotional and feeling beaten up, but together we gained strength and optimism. In just a short time, these two incredible women had become more than dear friends; they were like sisters to me.

Prior to going on the air, we prayed and said, "This is for the guys." That morning we did several national news interviews in a row. While the interviews with NBC, ABC, CBS, FOX, and CNN all blurred together, my memories are crystal clear of how the three of us snuggled next to each other and tightly held hands throughout the morning. Just like our three guys, the three of us were a team, focused on one outcome. We knew our men would be proud of us and the deep love we had formed for each other.

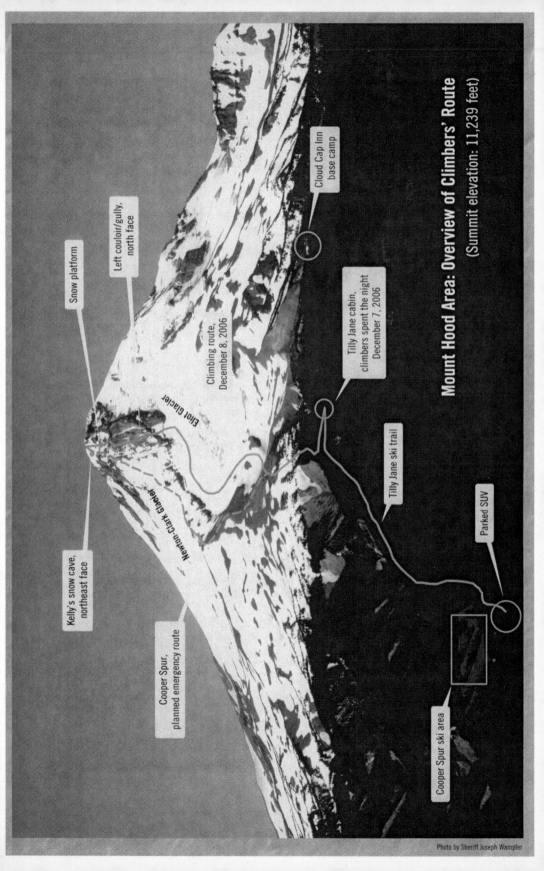

Mount Hood Area: Overview of Climbers' Route
(Summit elevation: 11,239 feet)

Snow platform

Left couloir/gully, north face

Cloud Cap Inn base camp

Eliot Glacier

Climbing route, December 8, 2006

Tilly Jane cabin, climbers spent the night December 7, 2006

Newton-Clark Glacier

Kelly's snow cave, northeast face

Cooper Spur, planned emergency route

Tilly Jane ski trail

Parked SUV

Cooper Spur ski area

Nikko looks on as Kelly adjusts his boots in the parking lot of the Cooper Spur ski area just before they start their adventure. (*Photo retrieved from Kelly's camera found in the snow cave.*)

The climbers left this note on the dashboard of their rented SUV.

Brian stands smiling in the doorway of Tilly Jane, anticipating the upcoming climb.
(*Photo retrieved from Kelly's camera found in the snow cave.*)

Kelly leads the way to the climb on Friday morning.
(*Photo retrieved from Kelly's camera found in the snow cave.*)

Nikko starts off the climb as Kelly snaps a quick photo.
(*Photo retrieved from Kelly's camera found in the snow cave.*)

Brian anchors the group with Nikko's pack on his back.
(*Photo retrieved from Kelly's camera found in the snow cave.*)

One in a series of several mountain shots taken by Kelly that helped the sheriff and investigators piece together what happened based on the elevation, weather, and daylight. (*Photo retrieved from Kelly's camera found in the snow cave.*)

Kelly's shot of the climbers' rope setup. The three-point anchor system indicates that the climb was very technical and very steep. No ropes can be seen above the anchors, which means that Kelly was leading the climb when he took this photo. (*Photo retrieved from Kelly's camera found in the snow cave.*)

Hood River County Sheriff Joe Wampler (*right*) and Deputy Chris Guertin
update the media on search and rescue efforts.

Search and rescue teams battle Mother Nature as they seek the missing climbers.

A C-130 airplane equipped with thermal imaging flies around the 11,239-foot mountain during the night, trying to detect body heat from the missing climbers.

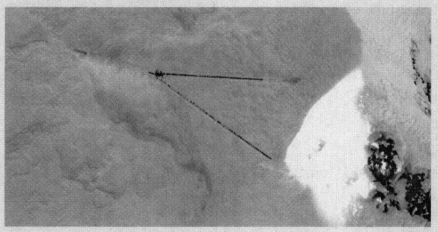

Seen from the air, this configuration was incorrectly reported by the media as a possible signal by the climbers: a Y outlined by climbing gear meaning "yes, we are okay." It turned out to be a cable anchor from a disassembled U.S. Forest Service cabin built in the 1930s to observe forest fires atop Mount Hood in the summer months.

Three sets of parallel tracks in the snow appear where the three climbers roped themselves together and made their way up to the summit from the snow platform. The elevation is approximately 11,000 feet.

Associated Press

Two sets of tracks in the snow are believed to be Brian and Nikko's descending from the snow cave after they left Kelly.

Associated Press

Todd Wells/Crag Rats

Rescue workers look out from a CH-47 Chinook at the summit of Mount Hood.

Todd Wells/Crag Rats

A rescue worker begins his descent from a Chinook to the summit of Mount Hood.

His backpack dangling from a harness, a rescue worker gazes down at the summit as he is lowered from a Chinook.

Members of the Air Force Reserve's 304th Rescue Squadron (*group on left*) work on the summit of Mount Hood. On the right is Brian Hukari, a member of the Hood River Crag Rats volunteer search and rescue team.

Brian Hukari descends from the summit to look for a depression spotted from the air. The depression turns out to be the snow platform used by the climbers as a rescue base.

Brian Hukari digs out the snow platform, which is covered with snow. The climbing anchor is seen here with a climbing rope attached to it (*left of Hukari*). This rope had been cut and the other half lies just below the platform. Under the snow at the platform, rescuers also found two short-handled ice tools, a gray wool glove, and a foam sleeping pad.

The three climbers used this snow platform at an elevation of 10,500 feet as a rescue workstation after their fall.

Andrew Siegel

Aerial view of the northeast side of Mount Hood. Kelly's snow cave is located in the center of the photo. The dark spot is a large rock and the snow cave is at the base. During the search most of the rock was covered with snow, which was later removed by the rescue team. The photo was taken after Kelly's body was airlifted off the summit.

Rescue workers prepare to enter Kelly's snow cave on the steep northeast side of Mount Hood, three hundred feet below the summit.

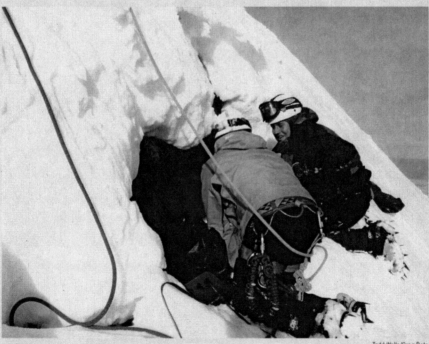

Staff Sergeant Derrick Brooks (*left*) and Staff Sergeant Josh Johnston of the Air Force Reserve's 304th Rescue Squadron enter the snow cave.

Todd Wells/Crag Rats

Staff Sergeant Josh Johnston secures the ropes on Kelly's body after it is retreived from the snow cave.

Josh Johnston

Kelly's body is lifted up the mountain from the snow cave on December 18, 2006, so it can be transported for formal identification.

A U.S. military Chinook helicopter transports the rescue team members
from the summit of Mount Hood after they find Kelly's body.

Snow cave,
northeast face (10,900 feet)

Snow platform,
north face (10,500 feet)

Left couloir/gully
climbing route

Three sets of parallel tracks head to the summit, then traverse south along the ridge as if the climbers were searching for the south route to Timberline Lodge. The tracks then move back out of the wind toward the location where the climbers dug in and built the snow cave.

Cooper Spur route

Two sets of tracks, believed to be Brian and Nikko's, leave the snow cave, go down, and dead-end at Black Spider above the Newton-Clark Glacier. The tracks then go back up and right, as if the climbers were looking for the Cooper Spur route. No other tracks were found.

Tracks Found on
Summit of Mount Hood
(Summit elevation: 11,239 feet)

Photo by Iain Morris, Portland Mountain Rescue

Associated Press

Angela Hall, Brian's sister, is comforted by Captain Mike Braibish
of the Oregon National Guard.

With the morning interviews over, power was slowly being restored in Hood River. Each new day brought new hope of rescue, but our hopes soon faded when we heard Friday's forecast. It was going to be another very difficult day. We had been there five days, and the climb started eight days ago.

Sheriff Wampler informed us that the forecast called for extreme conditions with wind gusts toward the summit as high as seventy miles per hour, with even more snow expected to blanket the mountain. They were going to conduct a limited search due to the hazardous weather and the extreme avalanche danger. Searchers would focus on areas below six thousand feet on the mountain to see if perhaps Brian and Nikko were lost or stuck at a lower elevation.

The sheriff was very concerned about the avalanche danger in much of the search area at the higher elevations. The recent heavy snowfall was barely clinging to the mountain, and it wouldn't take much to trigger a release. As rescue workers proceeded up the mountain, they constantly had to evaluate the threat of an avalanche, which slowed their climb.

But the sheriff, who also was a cheerleader for our families, quickly changed gears in an effort to keep us optimistic. He started talking about their plans for Saturday. He said they had an unprecedented response of resources for the weekend. Once again the sheriff said in complete amazement, "I've never seen anything like it before in my life. Every day we keep getting more people and more resources." We still had no idea of how big this story had become to the world outside our new home away from home.

Saturday, December 16, 6:00 a.m.

It was rescue day, and we all got up early in great anticipation of what was about to happen. I told the kids to pack their suitcases because we thought the rescue workers would get their dad and we would leave immediately to meet him at the hospital. I refused to have anything but positive thoughts. We had already been through so much heartache and waiting. I was ready to see my man.

The families met in town and then caravanned to the small Hood River Airport so that we could send off the rescue workers and the Black Hawk helicopters. Some rescue workers had already been on the mountain for several hours. Nearly seventy searchers had headed up the mountain, some starting as early as 4:00 a.m. The rescue climbers would approach from both the north and the south sides of the mountain. However, there was still a high avalanche threat. The mountain had been declared off-limits to recreational climbers above eight thousand feet so they could focus on finding Kelly, Brian, and Nikko.

There was also a total flight restriction for three nautical miles around Mount Hood, and only military aircraft and other aircraft helping in the search for the three stranded climbers were permitted. I couldn't believe the all-out effort that everyone was putting forward to find the guys. We learned that now that the Black Hawks could fly, due to the better weather, ground support was crucial for the air mission. Not thinking about their possible deteriorated state, I asked the sheriff, "When the guys hear the helicopters, won't they just come out?"

He explained, "They might not be able to hear the helicopters or might be too weak to venture out. That's why it's so important for the rescuers to be on the mountain to help them out if they need it."

Nearing the airport, I prepared the kids for what I had been told would be a large gathering of media: "Just stick together, and don't worry about the cameras. A lot of people are praying for us and Dad, and everyone wants to see the guys rescued."

Associated Press

A large group of media gathers for a news conference at the airport.

As we drove up, one of the kids said, "Oh, my gosh! Look at all the cameras." Understandably most of the kids were not comfortable with the media's presence and they had mixed emotions about being there, but they felt it was important to come along and show support of the rescue workers.

The night before, the families discussed who should address the media on Saturday, and we determined that it was time for people to hear from the three remarkable women who had remained behind the scenes the whole week while praying desperately for the return of their boys.

Each mother eagerly agreed to talk. They all wanted the world to know that these were their boys on the mountain and they were good men who loved God and their families. As had been the case with the other family members, it was also very important for the moms to personally thank the rescue workers for not giving up and for risking their lives to save Kelly, Brian, and Nikko.

With cameras rolling, Clara, Brian's mom, walked forward to speak. I remembered the special conversations Brian and I had about her. One night when Brian was helping me prepare the salad, while Kelly got the coals ready for the steaks, I started laughing and said, "Hey, Kelly has been making fun of you all week. He found some ABBA songs on your iPod. What's up with that?"

Brian started laughing too. Kelly was very into music and constantly made fun of Brian's music tastes, but ABBA took the teasing to a whole new level.

He said, "Man, I tried to hide those from him. But he saw them and just won't let it go."

We continued laughing, and then Brian paused and said, "You know why I have ABBA songs?"

"Why?" I asked curiously.

Brian got a wistful expression on his face and explained, "When I was a kid, I used to watch my mom sing to ABBA while she would do her hair and pick it out with a special comb." He added, "The songs remind me of her and make me feel good."

I was touched.

Looking at Clara in front of all those cameras, I smiled and whispered under my breath, "Brian, her hair looks good today."

Clara thanked the rescue workers, and then she said something that transported me back to our dining room table in Dallas: "Whenever Brian climbed a mountain, our goal was to look at the same moon. Last night, I saw the moon. We're very hopeful."

That was not the first time I had heard this. While we were eating dinner, Brian told me the same story. He said that no matter where in the world he was climbing, he and his mom always planned to look at the moon, knowing that the other was doing the same thing. It was a very special communication between this mother and son, and something both held dear to their hearts.

Brian's father, Dwight Hall (*left*), and the three mothers (*women, left to right*), Clara Hall, Maria Kim, and Lou Ann Cameron, speak with reporters.

Now seeing the moon brings a wave of emotion I could not have anticipated. For me, the moon will forever belong to Clara and Brian and symbolize their deep love for each other.

Then Nikko's mom, Maria Kim, a Korean immigrant, addressed the media and thanked the rescue workers. She revealed the emotions that all three mothers had been facing: "Every time I think about my son in a snow cave, hungry and cold, it tears my heart apart, but I know they are all strong men who believe in God. I know God is watching over them and keeping them safe."

Then in a defiant statement, she lashed out at the towering white force hovering above the news conference below. "I want the mountain to release our sons," she said. "The mountain has no right to keep our sons. I can't wait to hug my son, Jerry. Then I want to hug Brian and Kelly, my new family."

Yes, I thought, *we are all family, and these three men will forever be brothers.*

I was proud to see my mother-in-law step up, and I knew that Kelly would be tickled to see Lou Ann get in front of all those cameras. As this godly woman from Arkansas spoke, I could hear the depth of appreciation in her voice. Lou Ann was still very confident that Kelly would return home, and she said so.

But today wasn't just a rescue day; it was also Lou Ann's birthday, adding even more fuel to the family's belief that this had to be *the day*. Lou Ann told reporters, "It's my birthday and he wouldn't miss my birthday."

Kelly and his mom, Lou Ann Cameron.

As the three mothers concluded their statements, I was so impressed with their poise and strength. .

We were all eager for the news conference to conclude. While appreciative that people still cared enough to listen to us, we were tired of talking about a rescue. We were more than ready to see it happen.

We walked closer to the Black Hawks from the Oregon Army National Guard. They were planning to fly medics to the summit, and a third helicopter would join in the air search for the guys. We were told that they were prepared to fly them to a Portland hospital, and that was music to my ears.

The most beautiful sound in the world was the helicopters taking off. In my thoughts, I compared the sound of the motors starting up and blades whirling to that of Kelly's heart beating: *Surely he must know we are on our way.*

The families stood together and extended arms high in the sky with thumbs up. We had been waiting so long for this moment, and finally it was here.

What a country we live in! I thought. *These are just three regular guys, but their lives count to perfect strangers.*

Crews with rescue helicopters at Hood River Airport.

Day after day the pilots and rescue workers risked their safety to go after our loved ones. I was so appreciative and choked back the tears as the Black Hawks disappeared from sight.

Scanning the beautiful sky, I prayed the weather would hold. Saturday's forecast was dry and clear for the mountain, but the avalanche danger remained extremely high.

Saturday, December 16, Late Morning

Back at the EOC, Sheriff Wampler and Captain Bernard briefed us on what had happened overnight.

The rescue effort had continued even while we were sleeping. C-130 aircraft equipped with thermal imaging and heat-seeking cameras began flying at twelve thousand feet over the mountain at nightfall to see if they could pick up body heat from the guys. The pilots flew twelve-hour shifts, stopping only to refuel.

We asked the sheriff, "Did they find anything?"

"No," he replied, but he quickly added, "That doesn't mean anything bad." If they were deep in the snow cave, keeping warm, the infrared detection equipment would not be able to pick them up.

That's it, I thought. *Kelly is too deep in the cave to be detected.*

In the hallway, I overheard radio rescue traffic. I couldn't make out the whole thing but heard a portion of a conversation that said "located a target." My ears perked up.

Target. I knew what that meant. A helicopter must have spotted something that could be one of the guys. My stomach sank as I started to read more into that word. Is a *target* alive? I couldn't remember. I quickly reprimanded myself: *Karen, stop it! Don't do this to yourself.*

At that moment the sheriff and Captain Bernard raced out the back door.

"Oh, God, please, this is killing me. Please stop this," I prayed.

As I sat on pins and needles, Sheriff Wampler came back a short time later and said that the report was not of importance. One of the helicopters had seen two unidentified climbers at ninety-two hundred feet. From the air, they could see that one was standing and the other was lying in the snow. They could not tell if the one in the snow was injured, and when they did not wave back or signal to the helicopter, everyone started scrambling.

The sheriff said, "It turns out they were with the rescue team and were just taking a break. The reason they did not signal is that they have been trained not to wave at helicopters and look like they are signaling for help."

That made sense to me, but we were deeply disappointed again. I did not know how much more I could take of the cycle of positive and negative reports. Trying not to watch the clock, family members sat around the conference tables and exchanged stories about the guys. I was so tired that I curled up in a corner on the floor to try to get some sleep.

I had been talking throughout the day to Kathleen and Jessica, who were keeping me updated on what the outside world was saying. They had been working with Ashley to help Frank through the barrage of media requests.

Lying on the floor, I thought, *Bless his heart. Frank must be whipped.* Based on my experience, I knew how mentally exhausting it was to do interviews, and he had been on stage day after day. I was thankful to have such a wonderful brother-in-law and to have him there during this ordeal. I smiled and thought about all the trouble that Frank was going to give Kelly when he got off that mountain. I would just turn Frank, Lou Ann, and Katie loose, and Kelly would not stand a chance.

I reflected on Jack's comment about his dad being in trouble when he got back home. *Honey, you don't even know the wrath you are about to get from your family and friends,* I thought. *This climbing stuff is for the birds.*

Saturday, December 16, Late Afternoon

Sheriff Wampler entered the room, and things went eerily quiet.

I could tell it was not great news. The sheriff was very good at keeping his emotions in check, but after a week of watching and analyzing his every move, I was starting to get a good read on what to expect.

He started with the positive news that for the first time rescue workers were able to push beyond the ten-thousand-foot elevation line. However, the weather had taken a turn for the worse, and fifty-mile-per-hour gusts, churning snow, and near whiteout conditions had forced some rescuers to dig snow caves for cover and others to come back down the mountain.

But the sheriff was not about to send us away for the night on a negative note. He ended on a piece of hopeful news that gave us increased faith that the guys were alive and hunkered down. That afternoon, a CH-47 Chinook had spotted what looked to be a piece of climbing equipment about three hundred feet from the top. He added, "We have found anomalies in the snow that will help the rescue workers tomorrow by narrowing down the search area."

The rescue teams had zeroed in on their target, and it was just a matter of time.

The sheriff grinned broadly and stated, "Tomorrow. We are ready and have even more resources in place to get the guys."

Saturday was over. Tomorrow, Sunday, would be a week into the search. As I drifted off to sleep that night, I told Kelly, *One more night, baby. Just hold on.*

TEN

The Worst Day of My Life

Sunday, December 17, Early Morning

It was more than a week since we had spoken with Kelly. Time was running out, and there were reports that another storm was coming within the next few days. If it materialized, the search window would close.

But today we were optimistic. The weather was great, the sky was clear, our spirits were high, and we believed that a successful rescue was only hours away.

Once again we eagerly jumped out of bed and headed toward the small airport.

A sea of cameras and media was set up there. I thought, *They're like rabbits, multiplying faster than I have ever seen in my professional career as a reporter or public relations consultant.*

Getting out of the car, I glanced around and saw a reporter give me a thumbs-up. We locked eyes, and I returned his sign of positive reinforcement. For many of the media, it had become more than a story. They, too, were hoping for a Christmas miracle.

Throughout the week, several of the media had pulled Frank aside and told him privately that they were praying for our family. When Frank told me that, I smiled and thought that so many times members of the media are criticized for a vulture-like mentality, but that was not our experience.

I witnessed this firsthand. In two cases, well-known, seasoned journalists choked back tears while I was talking with them. One said to me, "In twenty years of reporting, no one has ever made me cry until now."

Associated Press

The families pray over a rescue helicopter.

After the interviews, I thought about their reaction and felt I knew why they were touched. The missing men were three All-American guys. They were your best friend, brother, son, father, and husband. We were ordinary people in an extraordinary situation, and many people had accepted us as part of their extended families.

Once again, the families participated in an early morning news conference, something that had became as common as getting our morning coffee. This time Brian's father, Dwight Hall, joined Frank in speaking on behalf of all the family members.

Frank addressed Saturday's unsuccessful rescue mission by telling reporters,

"Our emotions are running high. Our expectations are running high. We remain optimistic."

However, it was clear to all that after Saturday, the families, rescue workers, and even the media were emotionally tired. It was best put when Dwight said, "Obviously it's a roller coaster of emotions."

As we walked to the airstrip, we were once again warmly greeted, and someone asked if we wanted to see the rescue helicopter up close and meet the pilots before they took off.

We jumped at the opportunity. After seeing all the rescue and medical equipment, I thought, *Baby, you are going to be just fine.*

With all the families gathered around, Frank spoke up: "Let's put our hands on the helicopter and say a prayer." He said a wonderful prayer for the pilots, the rescue workers on the mountain, and the safe return of Kelly, Brian, and Nikko. It occurred to me that the helicopter then had a pretty powerful God force field protecting it and the crew.

Associated Press

I shake a rescue worker's hand as I offer him my thanks.

Seconds after I had this thought, the pilot of the other helicopter walked over and tapped Frank on the shoulder. After a pause, he said, "By any chance do you guys also want to pray over my helicopter?"

We all laughed, and Frank declared that the prayer we had just said was a blanket prayer for all of the helicopters. We then lined up to shake hands and offered words of gratitude to the rescue workers before they jumped aboard.

As I extended my hand to one rescuer, our eyes locked, and I said, "Please bring my man home to me." He paused, stared me deep in the eyes, and said, "That's what's we are planning to do." In that brief moment, I was connected at a very deep level with this stranger as he risked his life to save my husband's.

It was time for the helicopters to start their mission. Once again, I heard the magical sounds of the helicopter blades whipping around, and we waved as they took off to retrieve our loved ones.

Sunday, December 17, Late Morning

As we left the airport, officials of the sheriff's department encouraged us to take our time in coming to the EOC since they knew it would be a long day for us. But I wanted to be smack in the center of all the action and get there as soon as possible. Walking to the car, I could see the kids' faces and the tremendous toll that this was taking on them. They asked if they could wait at the bed-and-breakfast. I agreed and added, "I'll call you as soon as we hear anything."

Just like clockwork, Sheriff Wampler and Captain Bernard popped in to check on us. They outlined the plans for the day, and then the sheriff proclaimed, "It's a great day for a rescue." The room burst out in applause. Close to one hundred volunteers had mobilized for the day's search, and some rescue workers had started around 6:00 a.m. About twenty-five volunteers from Portland Mountain Rescue were heading up the south side of the mountain. A hand-picked search and rescue team was going to hit the north side. A Chinook helicopter would take off with members of the military's most elite rescue team, known as pararescuers, from the U.S. Air Force Reserve's 304th Rescue Squadron. Joining them were medics and rescuers from the Portland Mountain Rescue and the Hood River Crag Rats. The seasoned war pilots would lower the rescue team near the summit to look for the snow cave. Then the climbers would use fixed ropes to climb three hundred feet down the steep north face and search for the snow cave. Our spirits were also lifted after Captain Bernard told us that a test was conducted overnight in which a pararescuer dug a snow cave and climbed inside to see if he could be detected by the C-130 plane's infrared equipment. He explained that they could not detect the warm body, welcome news since the technology had not yet revealed our climbers. Now all we could do was wait.

Sunday, December 17, 1:00 p.m.

The sheriff returned around 1:00 p.m. and uttered the words we had waited eight long and painful days to hear, "The rescue workers are on the summit and working their way down to find Kelly in the snow cave."

Hold on, baby. You're coming home, kept running through my mind. I fought back the tears and could barely talk when I called the kids. Jason answered the phone and said, "Yeah, I know. We're watching it on CNN at the bed-and-breakfast."

At that point, the sheriff opened up the main command center in the EOC and let us all come inside to watch CNN. Together the families and law enforcement officials watched as the rescue happened live before our eyes on national TV. While the rescuers descended the ropes, my heart was beating so fast, it felt as if it would jump out of my chest.

The newscasters started talking about a Y shape in the snow. Commentators said that it could represent a signal from the climbers and it could mean, "Yes, we are okay." The room filled with cheers.

This anomaly was spotted by the CH-47 Chinook on Saturday and appeared to be a rope tied to climbing anchors in the shape of a Y in the same general area and elevation as the presumed location of the snow cave.

As I glanced over at the sheriff, he motioned me into his office. He had the pictures taken from the Chinook and asked if I wanted to see them. Of course I did. The close-up photographs clearly showed what looked like an intentional Y. But unlike the media reports being aired in the other room, Sheriff Wampler was not convinced that it meant the wishful interpretation of "yes, we are okay." He spoke carefully and cautioned that they did not yet know what it was or what it meant. His instinct would turn out to be correct. While rope and climbing anchors belonging to the guys would be found on the mountain, these were not the items pictured. The sheriff would later inform me that the Y reported by the media turned out to be a cable anchor from a disassembled U.S. Forest Service cabin built in the 1930s. During that time period, the Forest Service had stationed an observer in the cabin during the summer months to scan hundreds of square miles for forest fires. Due to high winds and snow, the Forest Service literally had to anchor the cabin down, but it kept blowing apart and the cabin was finally abandoned. The cable anchors and rock foundation still remain, and the cable anchor just happens to be right below the summit edge at the top of the gully route. The sheriff informed me that that he understood why the media misreported the significance of the Y: it looked exactly like a climbing anchor would look and was located in nearly the same place as the actual Y anchor used by the climbers.

Once again, I felt great appreciation for this man, his professionalism, and his care for us. Throughout the ordeal, he had grown very close to the families, and he was trying not to raise my hopes.

In another set of pictures, the sheriff showed me a rope anchor and a depression in the snow with tracks leading away from it. This is where the search crews were now headed because they believed the depression was the snow cave; the depression was also located in the same general area of the cell phone triangulation.

The sheriff then paused as he looked at a picture of a piece of rope. He said, "It's a clean cut. We can tell that the rope didn't break. And in all my years I have never seen a broken rope."

Staring at the photograph of the cut rope, I felt my stomach turn over. I had been a climber's wife for too many years not to realize its significance.

Upon seeing the reaction on my face, the sheriff stated, "We don't want to jump to any conclusions because we just don't know what it means. I just wanted to make sure that you saw this."

I went back into the room where everyone was watching TV. I was hoping that the Y did mean yes, and I was praying that none of the climbers was forced to cut the rope of a fellow climber who had fallen in order to save his own life.

Sunday, December 17, 2:00 p.m.

With one eye on the TV, I kept the other on the door. Kathleen would be walking in any minute. The previous night she informed me that the "gals"—meaning she, Jessica, and Ellen—had talked and she was coming to Oregon. I never would have asked her to make the trip, but after a week of operating on sheer adrenaline, I was starting to go downhill. I could use all the emotional support I could get, and I was happy that Kathleen was going to be with me to celebrate when they rescued Kelly.

Later I found out that my girlfriends had already talked among themselves about the unthinkable. They were anticipating the possibility of a tragic ending and could not bear the thought that I would learn of my husband's death without at least one of them being there to comfort me in person.

When Kathleen arrived, I introduced her as my best girlfriend. I didn't dare mention that she was also a national producer for ABC in fear that others in the room would not understand, especially since no member of the media was allowed near or in the EOC.

Kathleen and I have been friends for close to twenty years, and I trust her with my life. We met when I was a cub reporter and she was a news anchor at a TV station in West Texas. Throughout the ordeal, Kathleen shed her news role and worked hand in hand with Jessica and Ellen to help our family deal with the hundreds of media requests and multiple other issues. She was my friend first and a news producer second. I did not worry about any of the EOC details leaking out before the sheriff was ready to make an announcement. Just like viewers across the nation, we sat glued to the TV and clung to every word from the newscasters.

Around 2:00 p.m. they reported that the rescuers had found a snow cave. You could have heard a pin drop in the room.

This is it, baby. Wake up. You're coming home! But just as quickly, my excitement turned to complete confusion. The newscasters were saying that the snow cave was empty.

I looked over at the sheriff, who nodded, confirming what we had just heard. He said, "We just do not know yet."

A series of questions raced through my head: *Did Kelly get better and start climbing down the mountain? Did Brian and Nikko come back to get him? Where in the world are the guys?*

No one could move, waiting for the next piece of information. Then the newscaster said, "While there was no sign of the climbers, they did find two ice tools, a foam sleeping pad, and rope inside the cave."

That was very bad news. The guys would not have willingly ditched their ice tools. Ice tools are considered a climber's lifeline. There was no doubt now that someone was seriously hurt, something had gone very wrong, and they were facing more than just bad weather.

Sunday, December 17, 3:00 p.m.

Frank and I went into the sheriff's office to search the photos of the mountain. Perhaps our untrained eyes could spot something unusual. I was desperate for clues. In addition to the pictures of the gear, the sheriff had shots of footprints leading up to the summit, but the photos could not answer when the footprints were made.

While we were examining the pictures, the sheriff was busy in the next room with other law enforcement officials talking to rescue workers on the scene. Around 3:30 p.m. Sheriff Wampler heard from search and rescue on the mountain. They relayed a message in pre-agreed code words designed to communicate what they had found and prevent scanners below from leaking the news before investigators were ready. The sheriff could see Frank and me through the glass. He walked in, paused, and looked out his window. He then looked down, as if to gather his thoughts, and said, "I don't know how to say it any other way. I've got bad news."

Frank spoke up and said, "Just give it to us straight."

The sheriff nodded and said, "We've just found a body in another snow cave, and it is deceased. We don't know who it is and are trying to identify him."

Two snow caves? How could that be?

My head was spinning, and I felt sick. *Okay, I know this drill from my reporting days as a crime reporter. Give them as much detailed information as possible, and get this over with as quickly as possible.* With my heart in my throat, I blurted out, "Look for a JKJ signet ring." Kelly's full name was Jeffrey Kelly James, and he never took off that ring or his wedding ring. They would find this ring if it was Kelly.

The sheriff nodded and said, "Okay." He relayed this information to the rescue workers who were in the snow cave, looking for clues to identify the body that they had just found. The second snow cave was located four hundred feet to the south around the same elevation from the first one they found. We learned later that the first area they searched was not really a snow cave, but more of a smaller snow platform dug out to protect the climbers from the harsh elements and serve as a type of rescue station.

I told Frank, "I want to get out of here." I had to get back to the bed-and-breakfast as fast as possible. I dialed Jason and told him the news, then added, "Turn off the TV and don't let the other kids watch it anymore." Jason understood and said, "Okay."

Back at the bed-and-breakfast, I walked up to our room. The kids were lying down. The television was turned off, and they were just waiting. I feared that the identification of the body in the snow cave would leak out, and I did not want any of the family members to hear a possible false report. I crawled on the bed with Katie, and soon all of us were either on or around the queen-size bed.

Frank joined us upstairs. He looked at all of us and said, "Let's pray." He dropped to his knees and said, "God, please don't let it be Kelly. I know that by asking You this, we are willing it to be someone else and that others will be grieving tonight, but please don't let it be Kelly."

He said what I was thinking but was too ashamed to say. At that moment he was speaking as a brother. Throughout the ordeal, Frank had provided wisdom and guidance to all the families that we must trust God and His plan. But the horrific week had finally taken its toll on him. He stood before us, and despite all his spiritual wisdom, he was just as vulnerable and scared as we were. Frank had been almost superhuman during this event, serving as the families' spokesperson and providing daily counsel. But now he was just Frank James, and he was powerless to do anything else to save his little brother.

I prayed, *Please, please, please, God, do not do this.*

All of us went back downstairs. I can't recall exactly how long we waited, but the news arrived fairly soon. We were gathered in the living room when Frank walked back in. He was calm, and his voice sounded soothing as he spoke: "That was the sheriff. They have identified the body, and it's Kelly."

Immediately my eyes darted to the sofa where Jack was sitting between his brothers and sister. I will never in my life forget hearing the heart-aching cry of that twelve-year-old boy saying, "No!" as he burst into tears.

The room was spinning. We had to be in a nightmare. It couldn't be our lives. At first I couldn't comprehend what Frank had said. Did he just tell me that my husband and the kids' father was dead? The devastated faces across the room and the sounds of sobbing let me know that I had heard him correctly.

The impact hit me like lightning. I too began to cry and hugged everyone in the room. Then I ran upstairs and climbed into bed and curled up in a ball. I wanted Kelly back. And I cried out to my Maker, "God, what did You do?" I was forty-three and in love. "Why couldn't You give him back to us for Christmas?"

Sunday, December 17, Late Afternoon

Completely devastated, I felt the life drain from me. When Frank entered the room, he saw that I was in very bad shape, and he talked to me in a way that he knew I would respond. In a caring but firm voice he said, "Karen, you're a James. You have got to get up and go downstairs. The kids need you."

His words and direction immediately comforted me. That was exactly what Kelly would have said to me. I told myself, *Yes, I am a James. Get up.* I struggled out of bed. Frank hugged me, and we wept together.

For the next hour the family cried, hugged, and just loved on each other. Then it dawned on me what was going to happen next.

I turned to Kathleen and said, "Please get us out of here." Soon the media would be notified, and I wanted to get the kids out of Oregon as quickly as possible.

She got on the phone and worked with Jessica to find the first flight back home to Dallas. We were too late to catch the flight out that night, but we could leave the bed-and-breakfast, spend the night at the airport, and leave on a 6:00 a.m. flight the next day. "Let's do it," I said.

I explained to Frank and Lou Ann that I wanted to take the kids home. Lou Ann asked if we wanted to watch them bring the body down off the mountain before leaving, and I replied, "No, it's time to go." I did not resent the fact that the media would want a reaction from the devastated family since I understood that it was just part of the story. But for us, the story was over, and our hero was dead.

Then I remembered something. "Frank," I said, "you know Kelly's orange jacket that you have been wearing, the one that matches mine and the one he wore on Mount Rainer when he proposed?"

Frank nodded.

"I want you to keep it and think of Kelly when you wear it."

Frank swallowed hard before saying, "I will be very proud to wear Kelly James's engagement jacket. Thank you."

I then told the kids, "Okay, guys, you've got ten minutes to finish packing. We're leaving *now!*"

The kids moved like wildfire. They did not push back or ask to stay longer. Their goal was to stay together, and they too wanted to be far away from the place that had cruelly taken their father.

Within fifteen minutes the kids were lined up, the car was packed, and we were ready to go. A dear friend of Kelly's came over to me. Smiling, he said, "Karen, he taught you well. This reminds me of a Kelly James departure."

Just as we were about to step out the door, Brian's family—his sister, Angela; his mom, Clara; and his father, Dwight—came to say good-bye. They were joined by Michaela, Nikko's wife, and her best friend. They had heard the news and were coming to comfort us. They were crying, and when we saw them, the tears flowed freely. I remember their whispers, saying, "I am so sorry."

As I hugged them, I felt guilty for praying that Kelly was not the one in the snow cave. I realized if it wasn't Kelly, it would have to be either Brian or Nikko, and his family would be the one suffering tonight. And then I realized that they were suffering. We were all bonded through this tragedy and had become one big family. The death of Kelly had shattered their lives as well as ours.

We exchanged good-byes, and as I got in the car, I thought, *Oh, God, Brian.* In our grief over Kelly, I suddenly realized that since the other two climbers were not found nearby or hunkered down with Kelly, the search was not over. As Jason drove to the airport, we sat silently in the car, and I started to talk to Brian in my head: *D— it, Brian, survive! We can't lose you too. We need you! Kelly wants you to make it!*

We reached the airport hotel late, and the kids and I stayed in one room. The three boys curled up into one of the double beds, and Katie and I slept in the other. No one spoke. We were like zombies. I told the kids good night and said, "I love you guys. Try to get some rest. We have to be up in three hours, and it's going to be another tough day."

Monday, December 18, 4:00 a.m.

Kathleen called our room at 4:00 a.m. I was so thankful to have her with us. We met in the lobby and reviewed our next steps with the kids. I explained, "The media do not yet know it was Dad in the snow cave. I don't know if cameras will be at the airport, so just stick close and follow Kathleen and do what she says."

Then I was relieved to turn everything over to my best friend. I was running on empty and could no longer think clearly. Just like five little puppy dogs, we followed Kathleen through the airport and stood back as she negotiated our last-minute tickets on the earliest flight to Dallas.

Walking through the airport, I could feel the stares of those who recognized our family. I will always remember the tearful glance of the security worker who looked at my ticket and said, "We've been praying for your family."

Associated Press

A sign outside a restaurant in Parkdale, Oregon, solicits prayers for the climbers' rescue.

We were unable to get seats on the plane together, so I stuck the kids as close together as possible. Throughout the flight, I kept lifting myself out of the seat to check on them. I was in a state of total devastation, and sitting quietly by myself on the plane, reflecting on the loss of Kelly, was one of the most painful experiences of my life. I felt that I had died inside.

Monday, December 18, Midmorning

I glanced at my watch and realized that as we were flying home, Frank was getting ready to confirm to the media that Kelly was dead. Lou Ann,

Kelly's sister, Traci, and other family members had joined Frank for this last and very painful news conference. That morning, Frank told the world that a ring found on the body engraved with Kelly's initials, along with other items, had convinced the family it was him.

I was glad the kids and I were not there.

Looking out the window, I remembered that every time Kelly and I flew, he made the same comment when we hit twenty-nine thousand feet: "Can you believe this is the height of Mount Everest?" I just shook my head and laughed, saying, "No wonder they need oxygen."

At that moment, I painfully realized that I would never again sit with my husband and hold his hand on a plane and talk about the great time we were about to have on our next adventure. My trips, my dreams, my life with Kelly James were over.

The kids and I were thousands of feet in the air, and Frank was below, in front of the world, reading the most painful statement of his life:

This is a difficult day for all three families. Our hope was that Kelly, Brian, and Jerry would all be rescued safely and that has led these families to become very, very close. We're persuaded that Kelly has been found. But I feel like I have two other brothers still on the mountain, and the James family is deeply, deeply grateful to the rescue efforts to date. We wish the rescue workers Godspeed in their ongoing efforts to bring Brian and Jerry down that mountain safely. . . .

We find strength in your support and we join all of you in your prayers for the safe return of Brian and Jerry. . . . As Christians, we find peace that Kelly is with God. . . . Kelly always told us he felt closest to God when he was on the mountain. That is what drove him to climb. We find enormous comfort in knowing he lifted off that mountain from a place he loved, and from doing something that he loved very, very much. . . .

Thank you for all of your support. The family is very grateful.

Associated Press

Frank tells reporters that the rescue workers have found Kelly's body.

For a week Frank James had served eloquently as the voice of three united families. But for our family it was over, and that was his last news conference.

Kelly's body was airlifted off the mountain later that day, but it wouldn't be until a couple of months later that my mind actually let me connect that Kelly was in the black body bag.

Midway into the flight, I saw Katie walking down the aisle. Her beautiful eyes were puffy from crying, and her face looked stained from all the tears. As she walked toward me, she gave me a little smile. I immediately started to smile because I recognized that look. It's the same sly little smile her dad would give me just before he was about to be mischievous. When Katie leaned over, she said, "We've been talking and want to know if you want to do something with us."

I asked, "What?"

Katie said, "We are all going to get a tattoo of an ice axe in honor of Dad. Will you get one too?"

Laughing, I thought, *Wow, she is her father's daughter.* I never had a tattoo and vowed never to get one, but for some reason an ice axe tattoo now seemed quite appropriate.

I said, "You bet."

With that, Katie gave me a big smile and said, "That's great!"

As she walked away, I said, *Kelly, she needed you to walk her down the aisle when she gets married.* I started to cry again.

Our lives were forever changed. The world as we knew it, just one week ago, when we left Dallas, no longer existed. Kelly was the pillar of strength for our family and the person we all depended on.

He was gone, and I was lost.

PART 3

Putting the Pieces Together

ELEVEN

Operation Comfort and Care

WHEN OUR PLANE TOUCHED DOWN IN DALLAS, I COULDN'T BELIEVE WE were coming home without Kelly. I had packed a suitcase for him, thinking he would need more clothes when he got off the mountain. As I loaded it in the trunk of the car, nothing seemed real. I was in a state of shock and needed help.

Little did I know that this help was only thirty minutes away and would come in full force as my dear girlfriends transformed themselves into real-life superwomen. The leader of this pack was Ellen, my good friend, spiritual comforter, and backdoor neighbor. She coordinated a "rescue Karen" effort called Operation Comfort and Care.

As carefully as the logistics were planned, coordinated, and carried out for Kelly's rescue mission, so was the operation to bring me comfort in the darkest days of my life. Throughout the search, I had received tremendous phone and on-the-ground support, but that was nothing compared to what I was about to experience. I knew I had surrounded myself with incredible women, but it wasn't until I could no longer stand that I saw their phenomenal strength to carry me despite their grieving over the loss of Kelly. The love and support of my female network were unbelievable, and they were waiting to do what they did best—be great girlfriends.

The kids and I were silent driving home from the airport. In fact, the drive home felt eerily similar to our drive eight days prior when we left for the airport. We could not believe what was happening to our family. There was a big difference now, however. Back then, we had hope.

I dreaded entering the house. Thoughts kept racing across my mind. I wondered what it would feel like to walk through our front door, knowing that Kelly would never step foot again in the home he loved so much.

My friends had already anticipated how hard this first step would be. While we were traveling back from Oregon, my brother let them in the house to start the preparation for our return home. The first thing they did was to walk around the house and scan the rooms for evidence of Kelly. The whole house was a reflection of our relationship, but they wanted to make sure any small things that could trigger additional pain were removed from sight. One friend later told me that she and my brother just stood for a couple of minutes and stared at Kelly's bedroom slippers by the front door. They could not speak. My friend broke the silence and said, "We've got to put these in the closet. This is brutal."

With the house scanned for painful reminders of the ill-fated climbing trip, Ellen and her daughter, Shauna Archer, turned on all the lights and started cooking a comfort meal that I would never forget.

The closer we got to the house, the more physically sick I felt. I told the kids, "Guys, we are all going to do this together and walk in as a family."

Even though it was daylight, the lights were on, and as I turned the handle, I noticed the door was unlocked. When we walked through the front door, the incredible smell of rosemary filled the air. Ellen and Shauna were there to greet us, and they gave us long, meaningful hugs. Soon Jessica and Kathleen arrived to also comfort us.

Standing in the middle of our living room, I realized I had taken the first literal step into my new life without Kelly.

I have shared this first memory home with others because I felt so fortunate to have friends who anticipated what I would experience. It was one of the most comforting welcome home acts that I could have imagined. I believe it made a tremendous difference in the way I would view my home in the months to come. Ellen knew how traumatic it would be for the family to enter a cold, dark home, and she made sure Operation Comfort and Care started from the moment we landed in Dallas.

We immediately sat down and started eating the wonderful home-cooked meal of rosemary chicken and mashed potatoes. It was our first real meal since we had been gone. In Oregon we had survived on pizza and food that the sheriff's department had kindly provided for us in the EOC. The home-cooked meal was excellent, but I could barely swallow. The lump in my throat had not disappeared since Frank told us less than twenty-four hours ago that Kelly was dead.

SHORTLY AFTER WE ATE, JACK'S MOM PICKED HIM UP, AND THE OLDER KIDS went back to their own apartments and homes. I was thankful that there were other family members and friends to provide the love and comfort they needed. I had spent the last eight days fighting for Kelly's life and trying to protect them. I had gotten them to Oregon, watched out for their well-being while we were there, and then returned them home safely. That much I had accomplished. Now running on empty, I could barely take care of myself.

As I saw them to the door, I said, "I love you guys. I will call you about what we need to do."

Exhausted and numb, I felt as if I had failed to accomplish the most important job of my life, to save my husband's life. I had always worked very hard and, until then, believed that if you worked hard enough, gave it all the heart you had, and prayed, mountains would move. But the mountain did not move. In fact, quite the opposite had happened. It held on to Kelly, Brian, and Nikko so fiercely that all the manpower and cutting-edge technology could not break its wicked grip. Some might think it strange that I actually thought that I could get him off that mountain. But I believed, with God's help, I could make it happen.

God, why didn't You want him to survive? I wondered.

Then I sensed my friends staring at me. They must have noticed that I was deep in thought, and they were thoughts that no one dared to interrupt. I looked back at them and smiled. Just having them in the house was a comfort, and I did not want them to leave.

We didn't need to talk. In fact, there wasn't anything anyone could really say to ease the pain.

Suddenly the doorbell rang. I said, "Wonder who that is? No one knows we're home yet."

Jessica jumped up and said, "I'll get it."

Through the window, I saw a news van. I shook my head and said, "It's a reporter."

"I'll handle this," Jessica said firmly. She went outside and explained that the family just got home and was not doing interviews.

I said, "I guess they now know the body in the snow cave was Kelly."

Watching the news van leave, I glanced at the small rock hill across the street. It was Kelly's favorite spot, a special place where he would go and contemplate life and have deep, meaningful one-on-one talks with the kids.

Stop it, I told myself.

Everywhere I looked, everything I thought, was about him. It was so painful, I just wanted to turn off a switch and make all the harsh reality go away. But I could not.

We all knew that more reporters would appear on the doorstep. Because of the scenic view, Kelly never wanted front blinds. As a result, I could not hide from traffic on our street. Ellen, Jessica, and Kathleen pinned up sheets to provide some privacy.

I felt so exposed. My life and my husband's death had played out publicly in front of the world. It was as if someone had cut the center of my body and opened me up for the world to see.

My friends suggested that I try to get some rest. They knew I had refused all sleeping pills and drugs to ease the anxiety and pain while I was in Oregon. During the search for Kelly, I wanted to be as clearheaded as possible when the rescuers found him. I now needed something to take the edge off.

It was only noon, but I didn't care. I went to the bar to pour myself a large glass of red wine. With a glass of wine in one hand and Kelly's suitcase in the other, I went upstairs and walked into our closet. I slowly unzipped his bag, carefully unpacked all his clothes, and put them away in his drawers.

Alone in the closet, I looked up at God and began sobbing, "I just don't know what to do."

While I was upstairs, my friends discussed whether they should give me medication. Doctors had called, willing to prescribe the appropriate drugs to help me through this time. Ellen spoke up with definite thoughts on the subject: "We can drug her out now, but let's look at it this way. She can deal with it now or six months from now. Why don't we just keep an eye on her and see what happens?" My friends agreed. They wanted me to face the raw pain sooner than later and were prepared to be there every step of the way.

As I crawled into bed, I kept praying, "Please, God, I know You can do anything. Let's rewind this, and make it have a different ending. Please don't do this to me and the kids."

I loved my husband and loved being married to him. I had spent many years taking care of myself before I met Kelly and considered myself self-sufficient. While I had once prided myself on being independent, I had grown to love being dependent on Kelly to protect me, encourage me, and love me. Now, he could do none of these things, and I would have to get used to being on my own again. As I lay in bed, my girlfriends took turns sitting next to me, not saying much. They were determined not to leave me alone, knowing I was traumatized after spending more than a week on the mountain awaiting the rescue of my husband.

Also keeping me company was my cat, Caesar—or "Seizure," as Kelly liked to call him. To say Kelly was not a cat lover is an incredible understatement. But I had Caesar before we were married, and Kelly knew the cat was a nonnegotiable item. In his reluctance to live with the cat, Kelly imposed many cat rules, and one of them included "no cat on the bed." It was a rule that I was happy to break anytime Kelly wasn't looking. If you talked to Kelly long enough, his lack of fondness for Caesar was apparent.

My cat, Caesar. Kelly referred to him as "Seizure."

One day Brian's parents and I had a good laugh when we were in the EOC. They said that Brian told them that when he climbed with Kelly and they were in their tent, thousands of feet high on a mountain and just drifting off to sleep, Brian asked, "So where do you think the cat is sleeping now?" He said Kelly became irritated and muttered, "That d— cat!" Brian then let out a howl of laughter, knowing that I always broke the cat rules when they were away.

As Caesar snuggled close to me, he did not seem fearful that he might get caught. It almost appeared that he knew Kelly was not coming back. I remembered the night before Kelly left for the climbing trip. Caesar did something he had never done before. Kelly had all his gear lined up in the living room, and Caesar walked over to Kelly's sleeping pad and urinated on it. It was quite the scene in our house as I put my body between the two of them. I then thought, *Strange.*

As my girlfriends rotated shifts, I could hear the constant ringing of the doorbell. People were stopping by with food, flowers, and condolences. We had been home only a few hours, and it seemed as if the doorbell never stopped.

My friends put a sign on the front door saying, "Karen is only receiving family and friends at this time." Despite the sign, the doorbell kept ringing because people wanted to see me and talk about what happened.

Jessica came upstairs and said, "Karen, Michael's here and says he really wants to see you. I think he's a really good friend of Kelly's."

I thought a moment before asking, "Does he have really short blond hair?"

"Yes," she said.

Even in my grief, I was a bit amused and said, "That's our electrician." I added, "Everyone was Kelly's best friend. Can you please change the sign on the door to say we are receiving only *very* close friends?"

It was touching that Michael thought he was a close friend of Kelly's, but I was not surprised. Kelly had more friends than anyone I had ever met, and he was very sincere about his feelings for people. He had an incredible way of connecting to people, and he had an open door policy. Everyone was welcome in our home to sit a while and share a glass of wine and his or her life story. Kelly loved people, and people loved Kelly. As I drifted off to sleep, I thought, *I married well.*

When I woke up, Ellen was watching over me. I remembered her saying, "I am not leaving you alone your first night back."

Steve, Ellen's husband, had brought over her pajamas; he agreed with her assessment that I did not need to wake up at midnight alone in the house. With Kelly gone, Jack at his mom's home, and the other kids at their own homes, the house seemed emptier than it had ever been.

When I woke up, my pillow was wet; I must have been crying in my sleep. Ellen was stroking my hair, and I asked, "Did it really happen?"

Ellen's eyes welled up, and she said in a very soft, soothing voice, "Yes, baby, it did."

With as much energy as I could gather, I asked, "Why? We were so happy."

Ellen responded, "I don't know why. But God does. Right now we just don't know what He has planned. But He loves you and Kelly very much."

We didn't need to say anything else. There was nothing else to say. At least, that's what I thought.

TWELVE

The Last Interview

FROM THE MOMENT WE GOT HOME, WE WERE BOMBARDED WITH VISITORS, calls, flowers, and cards. Total strangers were taking time out of their days to write sincere and emotional letters. While on the mountain, we were out of touch with the news and what was happening back in Dallas and across the country. It was evident by the response I was receiving about Kelly's death that his story had touched many people and affected them deeply.

As I turned my attention to Kelly's funeral arrangements, I naïvely thought that once we were home, the media interest would stop.

But that was not the case.

We had been home a couple of days, and Jessica's and Kathleen's phones had not stopped ringing. Media continued to call, wanting to speak to the "grieving widow."

On Wednesday, December 20, Jessica and Kathleen decided to speak to me about the ongoing interest and discuss how I was going to respond to all the interview requests.

With only a few days before Christmas, the media wanted to see how the widow of Kelly James was grappling with the reality that the rescue was not a Christmas miracle.

Based on our journalist backgrounds, we all knew that the fastest way to shut down all the attention was to give a final interview, and then the media would go away.

While Kathleen and Jessica briefed me on the media interview requests, I became scared. I felt so raw and vulnerable. I was not emotionally capable of dealing with any criticism or attacks on Kelly, Brian, or Nikko. I wondered whether I could handle any interview.

A couple of hours later, Kathleen told me that Katie Couric was on the telephone. Katie was also a widow, and for the first time I could empathize with other women who had lost the love of their lives. I had become a member of a club that I never wanted to join. I agreed to talk to Katie and see how I felt.

Kathleen put Katie on, and we spoke a while. In this private widow-to-widow conversation, she understood my devastation, and on some unspoken level I felt that I could trust her to do a fair and compassionate interview that would not hurt me or the kids.

After I agreed to the interview, she asked, "Where do you want to do it?" I explained that I was not going to leave the house. After eight days on the mountain, I needed the comfort of my home to begin coping with the loss of Kelly. Katie responded, "No problem. I will come to you."

AT 5:00 A.M., THURSDAY, DECEMBER 21, THE FIRST SATELLITE TRUCK ARRIVED. Technicians swiftly started to transform my living room into a sea of cameras, cables, and lights. A row of producers set up at my dining room table and started typing away on their computers. They worked almost soundlessly. All of them showed an incredible amount of respect for me and my loss, and they did their best to make the interview as painless as possible.

When I met the photographers, I recognized one of them from a past work assignment. I had forgotten his name and could tell he was also trying to put the pieces together. Then he asked me, "So how did you get this assignment?"

I immediately realized that he had no idea who I was. I knew he would feel terrible when I responded, so I did it as kindly as possible. I said, "My husband was Kelly James."

The blood drained from his face as he apologized profusely. I actually felt bad for him as I thought, *Poor guy, that has to be one of the biggest faux pas I have ever heard.*

While I dreaded the thought of doing the interview, a part of me wanted to share more about the man that I loved so much. I recalled my reporting days when family members talked freely on camera about their loved ones who had just died, and I realized that my life had come full circle. Throughout my reporting career, I had competed for that first interview of the "hot story." Now the tables were turned, and I was the one facing the tragedy. Until that moment, I never really understood why so many people agreed to do interviews when they were grieving the loss of a loved one.

Now I painfully did.

The most wonderful man I had ever met had been cruelly ripped from my life, and as his widow, I felt an incredible duty to tell the world about him and the impact he made on earth. *After all, I couldn't rescue him, but I can honor him.*

As we briefly visited before the interview, I understood why Katie Couric had achieved her journalistic stature. She was a real person, who knew how to talk to real people facing real-life circumstances.

Going into the interview, I had no idea of what I would say, and I asked God to join me. I just couldn't do this one by myself. I knew it, and He knew it.

Katie started with event questions. Then she proceeded to questions that I imagined others might also be wondering. As a former reporter, I was surprised not by her questions, but by my lack of preparation going into the interview.

The grief was so strong that when the words came out, they were uncensored and directly from the heart.

Katie asked, "Is there any part of you that's angry that he did this?"

The answer to this question was a no-brainer. I never could stay angry at Kelly in life, let alone in death. He used to do a silly thing to me and the kids when we got mad at him. Kelly said in a playful way, "Don't you smile." After he repeated it several times, we couldn't help but laugh, and whatever happened to initiate the tension was usually forgotten quickly.

I responded to Katie, "I'm not angry. I'm really sad our journey is over, for a while. And I miss him terribly. But he loved life so much, and he taught me how to love. He taught me how to live. And I don't know how you can be angry at someone who loved their family, who loved God, and had so many friends and gave back so much more than he took."

As the interview progressed, Katie gave me a gift by asking a question that I believe every grieving person deeply appreciates answering. Kelly had lived a full life and, along the way, stumbled, as we all do, but in the end he had reached a place in which he understood his purpose and he had become the man that I was very proud to call my husband and friend.

Katie asked, "How do you think Kelly would want people to remember him?"

That was my opportunity to share with those who had watched the tragedy unfold on TV that he was not just a character in a story. Kelly James was truly an incredible man, who deeply touched many lives.

I replied, "Kelly was the biggest optimist you'd ever meet. And Kelly really wanted people to seize the day and he lived every day to the fullest, love as much as you can, live as much as you can, and appreciate people around you. And he's taught me that, and he's taught the kids that. And that's why I kind of feel I hit the lottery of life in men because I got to take a journey, and it wasn't long enough, but I got to take a journey with a man who just took me to the moon and back. And I'm very thankful for that."

Throughout our ordeal on the mountain, we never hid our faith. At times I was a bit surprised at the across-the-board news coverage on how often God was mentioned during the sound bites. I make this comment not in criticism, but as an observation, because I remember working in a newsroom and trying to be so politically correct that any mention of God became uncomfortable.

Since those days, I have changed a lot, and now I understand that He is the story and we are the supporting characters.

When Katie asked about faith, it was an easy question to answer.

"It sounds as if your faith was strengthened by this whole ordeal. But it must have been tested too," said Katie.

I quickly responded, "No, it was never tested. You know, I remember one time we were watching TV and he said to me, 'I can't wait to go to heaven.' And I said, 'What?' We were watching some show that had nothing to do with it. And he said, 'Yeah, that's going to be really cool.' And I said, 'You know, can you, can you hold off? Can we . . . can we wait?' But he wasn't scared. And so those conversations are what I hold onto."

Katie wrapped up the interview with a reflective question: "Is there any lesson for either other climbers or just for people in general from what's happened?"

As I thought, I answered with a message of love: "I've told a friend, a colleague of mine who I work with, hold your wife really, really tight because you don't know when your journey's going to end. And my journey ended with an 'I love you.' And . . . for others, if their journey ends with an 'I love you,' it's a lot to hold onto."

When we concluded the interview, I looked around the room. Many of the crew had been crying. I once again realized that many in the media were also hoping to see that Christmas miracle of a successful rescue and they ached for our family.

I went upstairs and woke up Ford and Jack so that they could meet Katie Couric. For many kids and young adults the sight of huge satellite trucks outside and New York producers sitting in the living room would have been a novelty. But Jack and Ford love their sleep, and even Katie Couric could not stir their interest enough to get up a few hours earlier for the actual interview.

After the kids met Katie, we all said good-bye. The boys went back to bed, and I went to my room where I started to become nauseous. Suddenly my heart was pounding, and I felt panicky. The impact of verbalizing my thoughts was catching up with me. In the interview, I had acknowledged that Kelly was really dead.

That was the first time.

It was also the first time I had talked so candidly about it, and the whole situation became that much closer to reality. With my head spinning I told Kathleen and Jessica that I couldn't do any more interviews.

They immediately sensed my pain and knew the interview had taken its toll. They responded, "No problem. It's over."

I once again marveled at Kathleen's sense of priorities. As a producer for ABC, she never pushed me. She knew I was at my breaking point, and she definitely loved me more than any professional kudos. I wondered whether my declining more interviews would hurt her professionally, but I had no strength to think about it further.

AS I CRAWLED INTO BED, I STARTED TO SINK LOWER THAN I HAVE EVER BEEN. Throughout my time on the mountain and since we had been back home, I felt God's presence. But that feeling began to disappear and was replaced by loneliness and darkness inside. I plummeted.

I painfully spoke out and asked God, "Why did You do this? I prayed so hard and I believe in You. Did You forsake me?" The emptiness was unbearable, and I felt totally lost.

In my anguish I began to sob. At that moment, the pain was so overwhelming, I did not care whether I lived or died.

Kathleen walked into the room to check on me, and as my friend of twenty years, she knew I was hitting rock bottom. I believe on some instinctive level she recognized it was a spiritual issue, and that's why she said, "I'm calling Ellen. I think you need spiritual help."

As I lay there alone, I kept praying. Then it was as if all the love, protection, and comfort I was missing once again started to flow inside me. The grief and sadness were still there, but I did not feel abandoned or desperate. It was a bit too weird to try to describe, and I decided that I would keep this strange event to myself.

That was until Ellen walked in the room.

She sat down on the side of my bed, reached out in a very motherly way, and stroked my hair. "How are you?" she asked.

I explained what happened.

She spoke words that I will remember for the rest of my life: "Always remember that feeling when you felt so empty because that's what many people who do not believe feel like all the time."

As painful as that event was, I received a blessing that day. I think God might have temporarily removed that incredible love and comfort I have in my heart on a daily basis so I would know in a very real way that He was definitely there and carrying me through the darkest days of my life.

I then asked Ellen, "How do people even get through one day without God?"

Ellen shook her head and said, "I don't know."

THIRTEEN

Home for the Holidays

BEFORE I KNEW IT, CHRISTMAS EVE ARRIVED. THERE WERE NO CHRISTMAS presents under our tree, and I had not bought a thing for the kids. It didn't feel like Christmas, and the thought of venturing out to go shopping and see the rest of the world, carrying on as if nothing had happened, was too much for me to bear.

I called Kathleen and told her, "I know I'll feel terrible if I don't have any Christmas gifts, but I don't have the strength."

She quickly responded, "Then we are going to take you shopping to help you buy gifts." She went on to say that she and her husband, Jake, would be over in an hour.

I agreed and said, "Let's go to the James Avery jewelry store."

It was the same place Kelly and I had bought our wedding rings, and the store that created his JKJ signet ring. I decided that I wanted the gifts to be symbolic and reflect our love for Kelly. While looking around the store, I found both male and female bracelets with Kelly's favorite verse of Scripture. The bracelets read, "I can do all things through Him who strengthens me."

Kelly had told me several stories about when he was climbing and felt that he was unable to take one more step or that he was in a perilous situation.

He would say this verse again and again. I bought different versions of the bracelet, in addition to plain silver ones, for all the kids, myself, Frank, Lou Ann, and Kelly's sister, Traci. The gifts were perfect, but I needed one more thing. We took all the bracelets to be engraved on the inside with "JKJ Forever." When I slid my bracelet on, I choked back the tears.

I was so excited to give the kids their bracelets that I could not wait until Christmas morning. After going to church on Christmas Eve, we came back to the house and gathered around the Christmas tree. I handed out the wrapped boxes and said, "I want you to unwrap these together. This is a gift from your dad."

When they saw their bracelets and the JKJ Forever engraving, many of us started to cry. With all of us wearing the bracelets, we decided to reach out and call Sheriff Wampler and Captain Bernard. A friend had confided a couple of days earlier that they were feeling very guilty about celebrating Christmas, knowing what we were going through. It took some time for the comment to sink in, but when it did, I realized that I needed to tell others to have a merry Christmas. They needed to hear from me that it was perfectly fine to enjoy this very special time of year with their loved ones.

Sheriff Wampler was not at his office when I called, so I told the dispatcher, "This is Karen James. The kids and I just wanted to wish him a merry Christmas." Immediately the dispatcher said, "Hold on. I will patch you through to his home." The sheriff picked up, and I said, "Sheriff, it is Karen James and the kids. We have you on the speaker phone and just wanted to wish you and your family a very merry Christmas." He was silent a few seconds and then responded, "Thank you very much. I can't tell you how much that means to me."

As we hung up, I remembered the words of Sheriff Wampler at the final Monday news conference when Kelly's body was being airlifted off the mountain. While being interviewed, he said, "We failed them. We literally failed them. But we tried our best. I know that."

When I was told what the sheriff said, I was totally surprised because that was not how the families felt. All three families knew beyond a shadow of a doubt that the rescue workers had tried everything possible to get the guys off the mountain. But it was just not meant to be.

It was dark outside by then. The kids said that they needed to go, and they asked, "What are you doing tonight?"

Although I am not one to tell untruths, I said, "I'm spending it with my family and friends. Don't worry about me. Have a great time tonight. I love you. Merry Christmas."

I saw them to the door, and when it closed, I knew I was in for a h— of a night.

The kids were not the only ones I had deceived about what I was doing. My family and friends had inquired, and I said that I was spending it with the kids.

CHRISTMAS EVE WAS A VERY SPECIAL NIGHT FOR KELLY AND ME. WE LIT A fire, opened a good bottle of red wine, and sat on the floor wrapping the kids' Christmas presents. Each year we reflected on the things that had happened and how lucky we were to have each other.

This Christmas Eve would be very different.

At first, I wasn't quite sure what to do, so I walked around the house and looked in every room. Maybe a part of me thought I could find Kelly, even though deep down I knew that would never happen.

The clock showed that it was only 8:00 p.m. I poured a glass of wine and sat down in the living room. Then the tears I had choked back all day erupted in full force, and I began to sob.

I was so overwhelmed with grief that I fell to my knees and screamed out at God, "Is this what You wanted? He's dead and I'm alone. Are You happy now?"

As soon as I said them, I regretted my words. It was the first time I had really challenged God, and frankly I was scared.

I immediately became quiet and listened. I wasn't sure what I was expecting, but part of me thought God would lash out at my disrespect. I almost expected something to come crashing down in my living room.

After sitting perfectly still for about five minutes, I realized that I was foolish, and I felt ashamed of my comments. Deep inside I knew God was not punishing me. Just like a parent hurts when his child is in distress, God was watching me, and He was sad to see me grieve. I was certain of that.

Part of my reason for spending Christmas Eve alone was that I had decided to confront this beast known as grief. I had always loved Christmas, and I was determined not to fear Christmas for the rest of my life. My thinking was pretty simple. I was already incredibly miserable, so I would face the grief head-on so I did not have to go through the same thing again.

I lasted about two hours and went to bed at 10:00 p.m. As I drifted off to sleep, I thought, *Tomorrow is Christmas Day. My family, Frank, and the kids are coming over, and it will be very special.*

But I wasn't that lucky.

At 3:00 a.m. I woke up ready to run a marathon. My heart was beating rapidly and I felt panicky.

With adrenaline rushing, I thought, *Okay, you feel miserable so let's just get all the miserable things over at one time.*

Kelly's funeral was set for two days after Christmas, a Wednesday. I had decided that we would have a video slide show tribute but had not yet picked out the photographs or music. Going through pictures was the last thing I wanted to do, but I knew it had to be done.

The house felt freezing. I turned up the heat, grabbed a cup of coffee, walked into Kelly's office, and dumped a large white plastic bin full of photographs on the floor. Over the next four hours I looked at every photograph and narrowed down the number that would appear in the slide show. It was a heart-wrenching experience as I relived our lives together.

At times I thought the night would never end. I remembered what Kelly had told me on Mount Rainier when my spirits were down as I climbed in the freezing dark. "Don't worry. You are doing great! When the sun comes up, your spirits will rise. I promise." This memory made me cry and I felt great comfort when I saw the sun start to rise out the office window. I was thankful the night was over. I had actually survived Christmas Eve without Kelly and even accomplished one of my tasks for the funeral. At that point I was measuring success by my ability to survive another night without him.

SINCE I HAD BEEN HOME, I HAD RECEIVED INCREDIBLE HELP FROM OUR church, Fellowship Bible Church of Dallas. Our pastor, Gary Brandenburg, had already visited me a couple of times. We talked a lot about Kelly and his incredible understanding that we all have a beginning and an ending date and it's what you do with the time you have on earth that counts. Gary once told me, "The statistics on death are pretty good. We are all going to die. Kelly knew how to really live with the time he was given. But most important, he knew where he was going."

One afternoon while we were talking, the doorbell rang. Gary knew that I did not want to talk with the media so he answered the door. Someone handed him a flower arrangement. The outpouring of love and flowers was overflowing, and we were running out of places to put the arrangements. I had already requested that in lieu of flowers, people donate the money to Mount Hood Search and Rescue, but the flowers kept coming.

Gary was just staring at the arrangement. It was artificial, made up of velvet red calla lilies with gold sparkles. It was very dark looking and reminded me a bit of Dracula meets disco. He walked over to me, held it out, and said, "I think this is a flower arrangement."

At that, I burst out in laughter. When I did, he started to laugh too. It truly was the ugliest arrangement I had ever seen in my life. For anyone who might recognize himself or herself as the sender, I want to apologize for that comment, but I truly thank you because that arrangement helped me laugh when I thought I would never laugh again.

Kathleen was coming over soon, so I strategically put the arrangement in a place where she could easily see it. As she walked in, I didn't say a word. Then she noticed it. All of a sudden she said, "What in the world is that?"

I replied, "It's a flower arrangement."

"No, it's not," she said.

I started laughing again. Kathleen immediately went into action and said, "I'm finding another location for this thing. Better yet, it's going into the garage."

Unfortunately it was a short-lived moment of humor. Kathleen got a serious expression on her face and said, "Hey, I don't want to ask you this, but I just can't remember and I've tried to figure it out by looking at photos. What side did Kelly part his hair on?"

"I don't know," I said. "He didn't really have a part. It just kind of flowed back." Kelly had great hair that was the envy of many of his friends.

Kathleen could tell I had no clue about why she was asking the question. "Sweetie, the funeral home needs to know how to fix it."

"Oh," I said.

Then she took me by the arm and said, "Come on. We have to pick out some clothes for him."

As we walked into our closet, I knew what to choose. I found the bright blue jacket he had worn when we first met. It still had a salsa stain on the lapel from an evening at one of our favorite Mexican restaurants.

"It's perfect. He would pick this," I said.

ALTHOUGH THE CHURCH HANDLED MANY FUNERAL DETAILS, I HAD TO PICK the plot and coffin. I asked the older kids to go with me. I had already decided to shelter Jack from as many unpleasant details as possible. He had been through a lot for a twelve-year-old.

I told the older kids, "I know this is terrible, but I want you to be able to weigh in on the location of where we bury him. I don't want you to be surprised by anything." Jason, Ford, and Katie agreed to go with me.

At Restland Cemetery in Dallas, we rode in an older white limousine to view available plots. I thought, *The last time I was in a limo was when Kelly and I were getting married, and now I am in one to find a spot to bury him.*

The driver stopped, and the funeral representative said, "Why don't you get out and I'll show you the exact location?"

As we exited the car, Katie crossed her arms, sat still, and stared ahead. "I'm not getting out," she stated.

"Honey, don't you want to look?" I asked.

"No, I'm not getting out," Katie repeated.

She was on overload, and I decided not to press her. I truly understood because if I could, I would have remained in the limo.

The boys and I walked around, but it didn't take long for us to know it was not the right location. There were no trees, and it was way too close to the street.

Part of me was already feeling a bit guilty about choosing this cemetery, but I was pressing ahead. Kelly and I once had a talk about where he wanted to be buried, yet I was never quite sure if he was serious.

While we were traveling through central Texas, Kelly showed me where his dad was buried in a little rural cemetery out in the middle of nowhere. He called it the "James Cemetery," but I thought I saw a sign that said "Possum Crossing," so that was how I referred to it thereafter.

With all due respect, it was the most unique cemetery I have ever seen. Surrounded by a rectangle chain link fence, it appeared to contain about forty graves. What made this cemetery memorable to me was that people put trinkets and objects on the graves to symbolize the lives of those buried there. One grave had a Matchbox race car and a beer can.

As I walked by, I thought, *Wonder how* he *died?*

On another grave there were all kinds of plastic animals. Kelly said that when he was a kid, they thought the woman was a witch doctor.

Another grave had a bunch of pots and pans.

I said, "Hey, I guess she must have been a cook."

Kelly quickly responded, "Don't worry, honey. We won't put cooking utensils on your grave." He loved to poke fun at my lack of interest in cooking.

"Very funny," I said.

Kelly took a deep breath, looked around, and said, "This is it. Bury me here!"

With my eyebrows raised and that "you've got to be kidding look" on my face, I asked, "And what do you want on your grave?"

Kelly said with a big smile, "Just put an ice axe right in the middle."

He was immensely enjoying my uneasiness that the site was being proposed as my final resting place, since we had always talked about being buried together.

"I'm sorry, but there is no way I am going to bury you here," I said. "Since I am planning on resting next to you, wherever you go means I go. After all, what in the world would you put on my grave?"

Kelly gave me that trouble-making smile of his and said, "We could always stuff Caesar, that cat of yours, and prop him up."

"Very funny," I said.

Prior to coming to Restland with the kids, I had spoken with Lou Ann and asked if she thought I had to bury Kelly at Possum Crossing. She laughed and said, "Definitely not. Let's keep him close to home."

With Momma, wife, and kids in agreement, I knew Kelly was just shaking his head in heaven. He would not be buried at Possum Crossing.

After being driven to a few more grave locations, I asked, "Can you show us something else?"

They explained that if I wanted two plots, one for him and one for me, the only things they had available in the area with the trees and water were double-decker graves in which two coffins were in one grave, one on top of the other. That did not seem a bad idea to me. *If I'm buried on top of him, I guess I can keep him out of trouble.* I was thinking how my playful husband, even in death, would respond to the notion of this grave setup.

Finally we came upon a beautiful location by the water. The boys agreed that it was the right spot, and I waved my arm for Katie to get out of the limo. Reluctantly she did, surveyed the area, and then said, "This is perfect."

TUESDAY, DECEMBER 26, WAS THE VISITATION. I REALLY DIDN'T KNOW WHAT to expect or do. Ellen sat me down and said, "Here's the deal. You're going to quickly learn that this night is not really for you or the family. It's for all the people who need to hug you and pay their respects to Kelly in order to get their own closure."

Ellen went on to say, "Your job is to smile, let them hug you, and thank them for coming. That's it. That's all you have to do."

What Ellen didn't tell me—and something that we had not predicted— was that an incredible number of people would attend the visitation. The line went out the chapel door, and I stood for a couple of hours greeting and thanking people. As I did, I felt comforted by the scarf around my neck. Kelly had brought it back from Alaska for me after he and Brian climbed Mount McKinley. Throughout the evening, I paused and glanced over at the closed coffin while thinking, *Baby, you were very popular and very loved. I love you.*

Kathleen and another special friend named Karen Boulle dressed me for the funeral the next day. Both women are very fashion forward, and Karen brought over every couture black jacket in her closet.

They told me what to do and I obliged.

"Okay, try on this one."

"Now let's put the pearls with this one."

I was in great hands, and I was so grateful to them since I was unable to handle dressing myself for such an unwanted event. My girlfriends had explained to me a few days earlier, "We don't want you to buy anything because you will never want to wear it again." They were right, and I was certainly in no state to go shopping.

At the church, I was amazed and touched by the size of the crowd. More than five hundred people gathered for Kelly's funeral. The music and words were incredible. But as I stared at the closed silver coffin, I couldn't connect it to Kelly. My husband couldn't possibly be dead.

Both Frank and Gary, our pastor, spoke. But it was Katie, Kelly's only daughter, whose words resonated with me most. I was so proud when the four kids joined hands and stood before everyone to honor their dad. Katie spoke for all the kids and told an incredible story. She explained that a friend of hers works with children who have cancer. When her friend heard about Kelly's death, she was very sad and could not conceal it from one of the children. The little girl asked her why she was so sad, and she explained that Kelly had died. It was the little girl's reaction that truly illustrated the phrase "having faith like a child." The little girl looked at Katie's friend, got excited, and said, "You mean that her daddy gets to be with Jesus on His birthday?" Katie then announced, "My dad is having the best Christmas ever." Needless to say, there was not a dry eye in the house.

At the grave site, the kids and I placed our hands on his coffin, Katie and I kissed it, and then we watched as it was slowly lowered into the ground. My thoughts on death had changed so much in less than ten days. I had become perfectly comfortable with the thought and, in fact, almost comforted by knowing that one day my coffin would be lowered on top of his.

THE DAY AFTER THE FUNERAL, THINGS STARTED TO SLOW DOWN. FAMILY went back home and friends returned to work. It was really the first quiet time that Jack and I had spent alone in the house together.

The first evening we sat down to watch TV, neither of us knew exactly where to sit on the sofa. Kelly, Jack, and I had our own designated spots. It was painfully obvious to both of us that Kelly was missing. Jack tried to compensate by sitting on Kelly's side.

I was trying to sound cheerful and make small talk, but I could see the tremendous grief on his face. I almost doubled over from the gut-wrenching pain in my stomach. "Hey, honey, I've got to run upstairs for a moment," I told him.

Escaping to my closet, I called a dear friend of Brian's. She is an older woman, also a widow, who once told me that she and death are old friends. I remembered that comment and in tears I called her.

"It's Karen. Jack is downstairs, and he hurts so much I can't stand it. I can't do this."

Kelly and Jack in 1997.

In a firm voice she said, "Yes, you can. Pull yourself together and you go love on that little boy. You guys will get through this together. You need each other. Go on. You can do it."

"Okay," I said. "Thank you." I wiped my eyes, splashed cold water on my face, and headed downstairs.

An idea occurred to me by the time I walked back into the room, and I asked him, "Hey, do you want to have a New Year's Eve party with a few of your friends?"

Jack perked up and said, "Yeah! That sounds great."

Kelly and I always loved to spend New Year's Eve with Jack. For us it was much more about being with family than getting dressed up and having a fancy meal away from home.

Despite his age, Kelly never outgrew lighting fireworks and running down the alley like a little kid. On both the Fourth of July and New Year's Eve, Kelly and the boys huddled together, planning something that they did not want me to hear. But I always knew what they were up to. Needless to say, setting off fireworks in the city of Dallas is not permitted.

One of Kelly's favorite pranks was to light Black Cats, fireworks with an extremely loud popping sound, right outside our neighbor Joe's house. Kelly then ran down the alley with the boys trailing behind, laughing so hard he couldn't breathe.

Back in the house, he said, "Everyone quiet. Joe's going to come out and get mad."

Like clockwork, Joe, a retired police officer, stormed out of his house and in a loud voice yelled, "Hey, you kids, you better stop that."

Upon hearing Joe, Kelly laughed harder. Kelly loved Joe, and I half suspect that Joe always knew Kelly had something to do with this ongoing childish prank.

Since Kelly would not be around to carry on the tradition, I decided that we needed a bit of Kelly James excitement on New Year's Eve. After I explained my plan to my friends, my wonderful girlfriend Tina Stacy showed up on my doorstep with sparklers and three fountain-type fireworks.

"I thought I would contribute a little something," she said.

I gave her a hug and said, "This is perfect. Tomorrow night we will light one each for Kelly, Brian, and Nikko."

In addition to these fireworks, Jason brought over a small arsenal. Upon seeing the bag, I became extremely nervous.

Jason could sense I was in uncharted territory and said, "Don't worry. I'll just let off a few."

"Okay," I said, breathing a sigh of relief.

As soon as it was dark, the boys followed exactly in Kelly's footsteps.

It wasn't long until we heard Joe's voice, "Hey, you! Stop it!"

Nervously laughing, the boys ran in the house to hide. I smiled and thought, *It's great to hear Joe's voice.* Repeating a familiar act made Kelly feel a little closer to home.

After an hour or so, we went back outside and lit the three fountains in honor of the guys. While the three fountains shot off beautiful sparks, I choked back the tears. That night, I could feel Kelly's presence with us. All I could think about was how much fun he was, and I was not at all sure that I would ever be that happy again.

After our back alley fireworks show, Jason left, and by 10:00 p.m. I could barely keep my eyes open. The house was locked up, and Jack and his friends had settled down in the TV room where we put sleeping bags so they could stay up and watch movies.

"Hey, guys, I am super-tired," I told them. "Come and wake me up at five minutes before midnight, and we will all celebrate and yell, 'Happy New Year!'"

At the appropriate time several twelve-year-old boys were trying to poke me awake and saying, "Get up. It's almost midnight."

"Okay, I'm coming."

I dragged myself out of bed and told them, "Okay, guys, everyone on the furniture because at the stroke of midnight we are going to jump onto the floor and yell, 'Happy New Year!' when we land."

The boys joined me in the countdown. "Five, four, three, two, one, jump!"

As you can imagine, that was a big hit. It felt great to see Jack having a good time with his friends.

Ten minutes later, I was back in bed. I could hear the boys giggling downstairs. As I drifted off to sleep, I thanked God for a good night. I had made it through New Year's Eve. It was now 2007, and the horror of last year was over—at least that's what I thought.

FOURTEEN

The Darkness

IT WAS A NEW YEAR, BUT I CERTAINLY WASN'T READY TO START A NEW LIFE. My brother, Karl, helped me spend most of January trying to get Kelly's things in order. My brother, mom, and dad felt his loss, too, and they pitched in to try to bring me some relief. With the support of family and friends, I thought perhaps I could put the pain of 2006 behind me. But

Left to right: My mom, Ann; my brother, Karl; my sister-in-law, Deborah; and my nephew, Dylan, feeding fish.

it was way too soon, and any thoughts that I was beginning to gain an emotional handle on coping with Kelly's death were naïve. I would soon understand that I was only beginning my long, hard journey.

Learning the news of Kelly's death, I was convinced, had to be the lowest point in my life. The family and I had suffered through eight agonizing days of praying for his rescue and safe return, only to receive the horrific news that he was dead in the snow cave. I had the

141

terrible honor of picking out his casket and his funeral flowers and then watched as he was slowly lowered into the ground. *Surely, this has to be the worst part,* I thought. But it was not. Grief is a strange thing.

Throughout the rescue effort and then burial, I was in a state of shock. While my mind was computing what was happening, my heart could not. For the first time in my life I had no head-heart connection. Over many months, I had battles with the Grief Beast. I had been grieving ever since the news of Kelly's death, but the Grief Beast would appear just when I thought I was beginning to comprehend what really had happened to my life. Without warning, he rode in, wielding the cruelest sword of all, and cut me in two. I knew it would take every bit of faith I had to fight and carry on.

One of my first big setbacks came in late February. The series of events that led to it started on Kelly's birthday, February 2, and then steadily progressed to the supposedly most romantic day of the year. On February 13, driving home in the evening from a business dinner, I started to think about what I should do for Valentine's Day. Usually Kelly made me a wonderful card on his computer, and I bought two cards for him from the local drugstore. One card was always funny and the other, romantic. Despite my new circumstances, old habits are hard to break and I still wanted to give something to my Valentine, so I stopped at the store. As I walked up and down the aisles, I saw other people looking for that special Valentine's gift. I desperately wished that my Valentine's Day would be the same as it had been in years past. This year instead of jumping out of bed on the morning of Valentine's Day and bringing back coffee and cards to my still sleeping love, I would be placing the cards on a grave.

Suddenly cards didn't seem quite enough; I wanted to buy something additional to place on his grave. But nothing in the store seemed appropriate because Kelly was not a trinket kind of guy. Nevertheless, I settled on a silly inflated small heart balloon on a stick and a tacky little white angel bear with a heart on its chest.

Of all the decisions I had made in my life, picking the perfect objects for his grave seemed to grow out of proportion in its importance and was weighing heavily on me. Not wanting to make a mistake and feeling unsure of myself, I started to fight back tears.

Then I could almost hear Kelly saying, *What in the world are you doing? This is no big deal.* It was something he would have said and then wrapped his arms around me as he lovingly laughed and I cried into his chest.

I made my purchase and headed home. It was around 10:00 p.m. as I drove up the alley. I hated coming home to a dark house. Except for Kelly's climbing trips, he was always home, and I could count on him having the music playing and walking toward the door to kiss me, saying with a big smile, "Hey, baby doll." With tears rolling down my face, I was again overwhelmed by the loss of the love of my life.

The cat greeted me at the door, and I let him out in the small enclosed courtyard to get some fresh air. About ten minutes later, I noticed he was not pawing at the glass door to come inside. It was a cold February evening, and Caesar was not an outside cat.

My heart sank as I thought that the electrician might have left the backyard gate open. I ran barefoot out the door to the side of the house and saw the open gate in the distance. I immediately started praying, "God, please don't let me lose Caesar. I just lost Kelly. Please, do not let this happen!"

Approaching the gate in the darkness, I could see my white cat walking down the street. Relieved, I ran through the gate and jumped down from a small retaining wall onto my neighbor's property. As soon as I landed, I felt a tremendous pain in my right foot. When I looked down and pulled up my foot, a board came with it. I had stepped on a piece of wood with a rusty nail sticking straight up. Operating on sheer adrenaline, I yanked the board and nail out of my foot. My only thought was to rescue my wandering cat, and I staggered over to pick him up, leaving a trail of blood along the way. Once inside the house, I immersed my foot in the bathtub, and it became obvious that I needed to go to the emergency room.

I grabbed my purse and drove myself to the hospital. It never occurred to me to call Ellen, my backdoor neighbor, for help. I guess with Kelly gone, I felt I was on my own. They put me in a room, and I curled up in a fetal position on the examining table and started to cry. How I had gotten from my house to the emergency room, I could not remember. All I knew was that I felt alone. If Kelly had been there, he would have been so worried about me, and he would have carried me in to get help. I desperately wanted him by my side. He always took care of me when I was hurt.

The doctor came in and, seeing my tears, said, "You must be in a lot of pain."

I looked up at him but could not respond. *You have no idea,* I thought. *But the pain in my foot is nothing compared to the pain in my heart.*

Leaving the hospital around 1:00 a.m., I hobbled back to my car, against doctor's orders not to walk on it. I had received a shot for pain at the hospital but was too tired to drive to the twenty-four-hour pharmacy to fill my prescription, so I decided to just go to bed. About an hour later, incredible pain awakened me. I tried to get out of bed but fell as I tried to stand. As I struggled onto my hands and knees, I crawled back into bed. I could not believe how overwhelming the pain was from having one nail go through my foot. In the dark, I could almost hear it throbbing.

I had reached a point of hating my life. I began to spiral into a very dark place. It was Valentine's Day, my heart was broken, and my body felt battered. As I lay in the dark feeling helpless, I told God, "You can just take me now. I do not want to do this without him. Please, God, let me be with him."

The Grief Beast was so unyielding that I wanted God to know that I was perfectly content to leave this earth if He wanted to take me. My husband could not be with me, so I wanted to be with him in heaven.

BECAUSE OF MY INJURED FOOT AND INABILITY TO MOVE AROUND, I NEVER made it to Kelly's grave on Valentine's Day. But just as I thought it had to be the worst Valentine's Day ever, the kids called and said, "We know this is going to be a very hard day for you, and we all are coming over tonight and bringing dinner." Their genuine concern for me filled my heart.

When the kids and Jason's wife, Sara, came over, they were surprised to see my condition. They had no idea about what happened the night before. Jack stayed by my side throughout the evening. Kelly's death had brought an uncertainty to our lives, and Jack kept asking, "Are you sure you're okay?"

Left to right: Jack, Ford, Katie, Jason, and Sara.

That night, we sat around the dining room table with one very noticeable empty chair, but soon the family banter and teasing, which up to Kelly's death had been a staple in our home, began again. Surrounded by the kids, I thought, *God, I understand that these are four really great reasons to keep pushing forward.* That Valentine's night I realized that I had been blessed with many different kinds of love and that God must have left me here for a purpose. I promised myself that I would regain my strength and go on.

UNLIKE CIRCUMSTANCES SURROUNDING OTHER DEATHS OF LOVED ONES, we also had to cope with missing friends, presumed dead. The fact that Brian and Nikko had not yet been found on Mount Hood kept the story alive and created constant anxiety and sorrow. Not to mention media interest.

It was a normal workday on Monday, February 19, when the phone rang at the office, and Jessica answered it. I heard the tone of her voice change and knew something was up when she said, "The family doesn't really have anything to say right now."

The only time Jessica used the term *the family* was when she was talking about Mount Hood. I asked her, "What was that about?"

Jessica said, "I don't want to tell you."

I asked, "Was it about the other climbers who recently went missing on Mount Hood?"

She nodded yes.

I had seen the recent news reports that three climbers and their dog were stranded on the mountain and a search was under way. Jack had called the night before to tell me about it: "There are three climbers caught on the mountain, and I wanted to tell you so we can pray really hard for them."

I had to choke back the tears. He was an incredible kid with sincere love for others. I tried not to let him hear the emotion in my voice as I said, "I am, sweetie. I love you very much."

Back in the office, I urged Jessica: "Come on, I know it was a reporter. Tell me what he said."

She responded, "It was disgusting." Not only was Jessica a tremendous business partner, but she was also a great friend who tried to protect me whenever she could.

"All right," she said. "They found the three climbers alive."

"That's great news," I said. "Thank God. So what did the reporter want?"

Jessica sighed and replied, "He said they found these three climbers alive, but Brian, Nikko, and Kelly are dead, and he wants to know how that makes the family feel."

"Unbelievable," I said. "Of course we are happy for them and their families."

It was a stupid question, and until then, we had been lucky to have avoided such media inquiries. Thinking the incident was over, we went back to work.

That night I sat down to watch TV at home. I turned on CNN, and Kelly's picture flashed up on the screen. The news was covering the recent rescue of the climbers and contrasting it to the fate of the guys in December. I just shook my head, turned off the TV, and went to bed. I cried myself to sleep, thinking, *Please, God, this is so tough. Please let it end.*

That same week was Brian's memorial service. Angela, Brian's sister, had invited me and the kids to join their family at a private luncheon beforehand and to sit with them during the service. We had grown to love Angela and Brian's parents, Dwight and Clara, as much as we loved Brian. Angela also informed me that Nikko's wife was flying in from New York. I was so excited to see Michaela. On the mountain we had had deep private talks. She was also madly in love with her husband, and we will always have a widow's bond. For both of us, our future with our husbands died on that mountain, and we needed only to look into each other's eyes to understand the pain the other was enduring.

That morning as I got dressed for Brian's memorial service, I felt sick to my stomach. I didn't want to do this. I was tired of dealing with the pain of death and still couldn't believe that we had also lost Brian. But I knew it was very important, and another part of me wanted to be there. It was also setting the kids back, and what little healing that had already taken place was being ripped open again. For the past couple of months, I had been grieving so deeply for Kelly that I had not had the chance to really focus on the loss of our dear friend Brian. It was now time to face another death in our family.

We walked into a packed church. So many people loved Brian that the church overflowed with those wishing to pay their respects and celebrate his life. As his friends paid tribute to him, I felt that Kelly should have been up there saying something. He and Brian loved each other like brothers and had life experiences together that took their friendship to a deep spiritual level. They had faced adversity while climbing and truly knew how to watch each other's back. Part of my admiration for my husband had to do with his tremendous loyalty and love for his friends. Brian was a part of Kelly, and Kelly was a part of him. Unlike my state of shock during Kelly's funeral, I was fully aware at Brian's service that none of the climbers would be coming back alive. Once again, three devastated families were together.

The impact from the service took its toll on me that night as I acknowledged that Brian was dead and the reality started to crystallize that Kelly was gone. I began to face the fact that the kids and I had lost both Kelly and Brian.

ON FRIDAY, FEBRUARY 23, AN IMAGE I HAD SEEN ON THE NEWS HIT ME LIKE a ton of bricks as I was driving to work on the freeway. The news video of the helicopter flying through the air with the suspended black body bag flashed into my mind. Suddenly it sank in that Kelly was in that body bag. I began sobbing so hard, I could not see to drive, and I had to pull over onto the side of the freeway.

With the realization of Kelly's death now unleashed on all emotional levels, the Grief Beast and I officially entered into combat. Grief was a fierce opponent that could strike anywhere at any time. Instead of being afraid of it, I decided to declare war and prayed for God to give me the strength to overcome its suffocating grip.

With time and prayer, the physical, sick feeling of grief that I felt in the first few months subsided into a sorrowful sense of loss. Rather than having to fight the pain, I became more reflective on what I had lost, and my sadness deepened. This new phase of grief had its own set of side effects. Instead of being apprehensive about when grief would strike, I started to feel trapped in sorrow.

There were nights when I sat on the sofa by myself and reached out to stroke Kelly's head as I had done hundreds of times before. I knew he was not there, but I had the strong desire to repeat a familiar, comforting behavior. Every night he sat in the same spot on the sofa, and physically reaching out to him seemed perfectly natural despite the obvious fact that his seat was very much empty. Soon this phase passed too.

I HAD STILL NOT EXPERIENCED MY MOST SIGNIFICANT CONFRONTATION with his death. That came the first time I went to his grave alone, three months after his death. I had not planned a graveside visit, but decided to go after I got lost looking for a store and found myself just one street over from the cemetery.

It was a beautiful day, a vivid contrast to the brutal weather that claimed his life. I slowly walked up to Kelly's grave and decided to sit down and spend some time. Some of the turned over dirt hadn't quite settled down from his burial.

Then a very dark thing happened. It dawned on me that he was only a few feet away, and a sensation took over my body. I wanted to get him out of there, and for a split second I wanted to reach out and start clawing at the dirt. I felt once again he was trapped. First it was the snow cave, and now it was his grave. He wasn't supposed to be there under that dirt. I still wanted to rescue him and bring him home to me. It wasn't right.

I pleaded to God to do something that I knew would never happen. I begged, "God, please! I believe You are a God of miracles. I know Jesus raised Lazarus from the dead, so why can't You raise Kelly?" Even as I said it, I knew what I was asking was crazy, but in that moment of desperation to get my husband back, I wanted to pull out all the stops and confront God with everything I had learned was in His capability. After I said this, I felt foolish.

While I knew God was listening, I believed that He was not going to participate in this conversation. He loved me and was there with me, but He was watching more as a loving parent when a child falls down to see if she will try to get up on her own. As I sat on Kelly's grave, the tears flowing freely, my mind drifted back to the visitation the evening before Kelly's funeral.

That night, we opened the casket for a short time for family only. I was unsure about looking closely at Kelly. It had been suggested to me that the harsh weather conditions had taken a toll on his body. From across the room, I could see his beautiful hair, and he looked as if he was peacefully sleeping. I asked Frank whether he would help me and look at Kelly first. That put an incredible burden on him, but he was willing to shoulder it and I was grateful. Since the kids and I were flying back to Dallas as they were taking Kelly's body off the mountain, Frank remained at the mountain to formally identify him for officials. While Lou Ann had requested to do it, Frank wanted to protect his mother and stepped in to take that burden alone.

The reactions of the rest of the family after viewing Kelly's body did not lessen my inner turmoil. I sat there with Jack next to my side and said, "I don't know what to do yet. Let's wait to see what Uncle Frank says. We'll do this together."

Frank came back from viewing Kelly and kneeled down between Jack and me. He said to us, "I would recommend that you do not go look at Kelly. He does not look like himself, and I am worried about the impact it will have on you guys."

Jack looked down, shook his head, and said, "I don't want to look."

I asked him, "Are you sure?"

He nodded and said, "Yes."

I said, "Okay. Then I'm staying right here with you. If you don't want to look, I don't want to look either."

Frank told us, "I think that's a great idea."

Now as I looked down at Kelly's grave, I was once again grateful for Frank's guidance. I know that was the best decision for me and, I also believe, for Jack. My last memory of seeing Kelly will always be him kissing me good-bye to leave for the airport and saying, "I love you very much and will see you on Monday."

D——, I thought. *You looked me right in the eyes and promised you would never leave me. Why did you have to die?*

I stared at the plot of dirt that was now Kelly's earthly resting place and felt completely drained. It was as if all the love and life had been sucked out of me, and I was a walking shell.

Wiping my eyes, I stood up and slowly walked back to my car. I turned around and whispered, "Good-bye." Despite the excruciating pain, I knew by the mere fact that I had made it this far, I was going to get through this.

THROUGHOUT THE SPRING, I WAS FUNCTIONING DURING THE DAY BY immersing myself in work, but after hours, it was a very different story. It was almost May, and I was getting to the point where I could go through a day without crying—that is, until a large package appeared on my doorstep. After months of waiting, we had finally received Kelly's belongings from the snow cave. I called all the kids and told them that the package had arrived, and I would wait to open it until we were all together two days later.

I tried to go on about my day, but I couldn't keep from staring at the large box now sitting in the middle of the living room. At times it was as if the big brown box called to me, and I circled it, wondering whether seeing its contents would be painful to me, whether there would be any surprises when we opened it.

As these thoughts consumed me, I started to spiral downward, and by 7:00 p.m. I'd had enough. I crawled into bed and once again put the covers over my head. I thought sleep would be my best escape. Around 2:00 a.m. I woke up with Kelly on my mind. Caesar was next to me, enjoying his newfound freedom, lying on the bed. As he purred, I thought about the late nights that Kelly spent in the home office below our bedroom as he worked on a landscaping project. When I woke up and realized that he was still working at a late hour, I called out to him to come to bed. I wondered what it would sound like to hear his name. Part of me wanted to call for him. Did I dare?

Suddenly I sat up in bed and yelled loudly, "Kelly, come to bed." To my surprise, Caesar jumped up in a panic. With ears straight back, he started to look around for him. He knew exactly whom I was calling, and his posture showed that he was fearful he would be in trouble for being in the bed. Doing such a thing seemed strange, but Caesar's reaction curiously comforted me. In a way it seemed like old times, Kelly versus the cat. Oh, how I missed him! The bed felt so empty.

That next day was Wednesday, and the kids were coming over. Since I had met Kelly, Wednesday night was family night, and I happily embraced this tradition after we were married. Over the years, while Jack, Kelly, and I were always together for dinner, the older kids' attendance would waver based on their work and social calendars. Since Kelly's death, I had seen a renewed commitment from the older kids in being together for dinner. They knew that Kelly would want us to stick together, and being there for Jack had taken top priority in all our lives. We were also united in our commitment to keeping things as normal as possible for Jack. Opening the box would make it a tough night, so I decided to make a day of it and also finalize the memorial marker before we got together.

That afternoon I went to the funeral home to lock down the wording on the grave plaque. Since I had chosen a double grave so I could be buried with Kelly, I was also planning what my own plaque would look like. The whole thing seemed bizarre. I had been working over the past month with the funeral representative on designing the plaque. In the course of our discussions she told me that, in many cases, they put the surviving spouse's name on the marker with the birth date and then just filled in the death date when that day arrived. I really didn't know how to respond. I took a girlfriend poll about what to do. I had to laugh at their reaction when the poll came back unanimously no. They were not going to let me visit Kelly's grave and each time see my name on the grave marker. We decided it would be added after my death.

With that decision made, I thought very hard about the words on the marker, which I wanted to honor my husband. I drafted the words and shared them with Lou Ann, Frank, and the kids. I wanted to make sure that everyone felt good about the wording. Frank commented that he liked it, but the word *phenomenal* wasn't typical wording. I had to laugh at the subtle "are you sure you want to do that?" tone in his voice. Chuckling, I responded, "I know, but Kelly wasn't your typical man, He *was* phenomenal." Frank quickly said, "I agree with that. He was phenomenal. Go for it."

At the funeral home office, I signed off on the wording that would mark our earthly resting place. The words below Kelly's grave read, *Phenomenal Husband, Dad, Son, Brother, Friend, Mountaineer and Christian.* I added a personal note: *Thank you for taking me to the moon and back. Love Forever, Karen.* On the marker I chose a picture of a mountain and his favorite verse from Scripture: *I can do all things through Him who strengthens me. Philippians 4:13.* I knew it was right.

Getting ready to leave, I bumped into one of the men who coordinated the

Kelly's grave marker.

funeral, and he said, "I have a box of Kelly's things. Do you want them?" I was shocked. Another box? Of course I said, "Yes!" He brought me the box, which was full of the clothes Kelly was wearing when he died. His blue climbing jacket was sticking out of it. I asked if I could have a few minutes alone. I grabbed the jacket and buried my face in it. It felt so good and so familiar. I had buried my head on his chest and snuggled up to him in this jacket so many times. Once more the cold reality hit me hard. I had the jacket, but the man I loved was not there wearing it. I burst into tears.

Leaving the room, I decided to

drive to Kelly's grave because I wanted to show him that I had his jacket. As I started to load the box of his belongings in the backseat, I noticed a six-inch horizontal rip on the back of his climbing jacket. I had not seen it in the office when I picked it up the first time. I put the jacket on the hood of my car, the wind picked up, and dozens of down feathers started flying around me. I frantically started to grab them to put them back inside. I then stopped cold. I realized that Kelly would never need his jacket again or the feathers that were flying beyond my reach. I thought, *Give it up. I will just put a piece of duct tape on the back when I get home.* Kelly always said that duct tape was one of man's greatest inventions, and he used it for so many things that I was sure the inventor had never imagined.

At Kelly's grave, I kneeled down next to the temporary marker spelling out his name, and I told him, "Baby, I have your jacket and I'm taking it home."

I wasn't sure the tears would ever stop. I believe that only someone who has grieved can truly understand the depth of emotion. I prayed for strength as I drove home to meet the kids. We had another box to open.

FIFTEEN

So What Really Happened?

EVEN BEFORE WE KNEW KELLY'S FATE, I WAS BUSY SEARCHING FOR CLUES about what happened on the mountain. The process began Sunday, December 10, when we first learned that Kelly, Brian, and Nikko were missing.

I had immediately raced home and started going through Kelly's e-mail. Throughout the months leading up to the climb, Kelly, Brian, and Nikko had left a long string of e-mails detailing their route and equipment. After reading through months of correspondence, I had no doubt that the three climbers had done their homework. Their attention to detail was impressive, but what really touched me was the friendship evident in their discussions. Their male banter made me laugh. These guys were excited for their adventure together and committed to a successful and safe climb. Here are examples:

From: Kelly James
To: Jerry Cooke
Subject: Re: Mount Hood North Face first week of December
Date: Fri, 01 Sep 2006 17:58:38

We're in brother, can we go Dec. 6-10? . . . looks like a great climb, I have climbed Hood before years ago on the backside, not sure the route name.

Brian is excited and so am I, so count us in.

Let's discuss all the particulars soon.

From: Jerry Cooke
To: Kelly James
Subject: Re: Mount Hood North Face first week of December
Date: Mon, 04 Sep 2006 08:40:19

Kelly:

I knew you guys would bite, it's just too easy a trip to squeeze in for the end of the year. Give us till next week, I think 12/6-12/10 works fine for me, gotta check on Willy. He's not married yet so he has lots more leverage than you or me!

Logistics wise once we are 100% on the dates we can talk about tickets.

I'll give you a call next weekend and we can sort out the flights, climbing eqt., etc.

As I read their correspondence, I was feeling good until I saw an e-mail that Nikko sent on September 7, 2006. The words he wrote three months prior to the climb—"won't have to risk descending in darkness down the south side (or worse)"— now seemed prophetic and sent a chill down my spine.

From: Jerry Cooke
To: Kelly James, Brian Hall
Subject: Re: Mount Hood Details
Date: Thu, 07 Sep 2006 10:04:54

Kelly & Brian—

Ok guys I am 100% . . .

I have all we need in terms of ice gear EXCEPT two 10cm ice screws . . .

I guess we have 2 options, either bivy at the base of the climb and climb the next morning or try to do it all in one long day.

While weather and snow conditions may make these decisions for us just wondering if you prefer the sound of one over the other? I like the idea of a bivy since we are all coming from sea level and one night at 8500' before going for the summit sounds reasonable. Also we will . . . be at the ice pitches by dawn, and won't have to risk descending in darkness down the south side (or worse).

Anyway unless you guys tell me you are 100% against the idea of a bivy I will buy a bivy sac so I can roll with the Texas hardmen.

I am happy to stay wherever and whenever you guys want as far as hotel/motel in Portland. I will take my own room so you guys can share one (and since Brian snores).

From September to just a couple of days before they headed for the mountain in the first week of December, the three climbers left no stone unturned in their discussions about equipment and logistics. Their excitement never wavered.

From: Jerry Cooke
To: Kelly James, Brian Hall
Subject: Mt Hood, y'all
Date: Sun, 17 Sep 2006 16:35:01

Nothing particular, just excited for the climb, thought I'd give you guys an e-mail shout between the Yankees-Sox doubleheader.

Brian—the Mt. Hood Timberline Lodge is only 60 miles from Portland.

It's really cool because we will have 3 full days to do the climb, we should get favorable conditions in there somewhere.

I'm going to post some questions on cascadeclimbers.com today in the Oregon Cascades section.

Hope the Astros make the playoffs and eliminate the Mets in the 1st round.
Nikko

From: Jerry Cooke
To: Kelly James
CC: Brian Hall
Subject: last minute details
Date: Mon, 04 Dec 2006 13:56:19

Kelly:

Just got off the phone with REI Portland. Good news they have bivy in stock so I can buy one and bring it along.

Since Brian's buddy is gonna meet us by Timberline, that means we can just stop at REI from the airport, get fuel, food, snowshoes, whatever, then go directly to the North side of the Mt. if we want.

See ya Weds.

On Wednesday morning, December 6, Kelly and Brian boarded a flight to meet Nikko for their much anticipated adventure.

It would be the last time I would see Kelly alive.

Putting the pieces together of what happened on their climb would take time, but I was able to fill in the gaps, based on my conversations with Kelly prior to his trip, the photographs taken on his camera, the last calls placed on his recovered cell phone, and the items Kelly, Brian, and Nikko stashed just prior to their climb. Kelly's death certificate also revealed a potential clue that was originally dismissed in earlier news reports.

Initially we operated off the theory that the sheriff and rescue workers had proposed immediately after Kelly's body was discovered. But after taking a closer look at the evidence and having further talks with Sheriff Wampler, I was later able to painfully understand the dramatic events that unfolded in December 2006 on Mount Hood.

So What Really Happened?

The first working theory was officially announced on Monday, December 18, the same day Kelly's body was airlifted off the mountain, when Sheriff Wampler made a statement to reporters on what investigators thought happened to the climbers.

This is what we surmised happened on Mt. Hood. We think the three climbers left Tilly Jane . . . and climbed . . . the right gully to the summit of Mt. Hood and that they actually summited. When they got to the summit . . . this is where we are guessing now because of footprints, it looks like they went South along the summit ridge of Mt. Hood maybe looking for the entrance to the Pearly Gates which is the route back down that they had planned on doing. Somehow because of weather, probably visibility, they did not get down that way. They were right there at top of it but instead broke off to the east side of the mountain, all three together, dropped down about 300 feet . . . below the summit . . . dug a cave that probably housed all three of them on the Friday night. Then probably Saturday morning it looks like two of those climbers left that cave, went back to the north just below the summit ridge . . . their intention was in case something went wrong to descend the Cooper Spur route which was virtually right next to the place where they had climbed up but now the weather is getting bad and it was pretty obvious because they were having to dig in. So now we got two climbers working their way back to where they came. And now you are talking about a point on the mountain that can go anywhere. Because there was an anchor with a snow cave, more like a shelter since it wasn't a good snow cave like the first one they built where the body is, it's more like a place that they cut out of the snow on the steep hillside to work from since it had two aluminum snow anchors driven in the snow with some webbing that told us while they were there they put something in the snow so they would be safe since there were two slings coming off that indicates two people used their carabineers to clip in for the purpose of just being stable on a steep slope of the mountain. At that point there were some ices axes found. Two short handheld ice axes both exactly the same, so we can assume that was the property of one climber, right there was a little a piece of foam sleeping pad, there wasn't a sleeping bag, there was one wool glove, a piece of rope so we can only assume that was the last known location of two of the climbers . . . historically we have had a lot of problems in this area in the event of a fall.

As I set out on my personal journey to discover what happened, it appeared from the very beginning of the trip that, despite the steps the guys took, they were destined to encounter the storm of a decade.

I started piecing the puzzle together with the trail of notes the guys left before their climb. From the note in the SUV parked at the trailhead at the Cooper Spur ski area, I could tell immediately they had changed their plans.

The picture captured on Kelly's camera just before they left the ski lodge parking lot shows him in full climber mode, adjusting his boots with a fully packed backpack. Nikko stands watching him, ready and eager to go.

While the picture of Kelly looked normal, the note on the dashboard contained two details that were anything but normal based on the conversation I had with Kelly just before he left for Oregon. The timing and the addition of a route for an "emergency storm" caught my eye.

On Monday, December 4, Kelly and I sat in our living room in front of the fire and talked in detail about their plans. This conversation would come back to haunt me because in their note, they referenced "sleep 12/7," which was Thursday night, and "descend south side on Friday." This indicated only one night on the mountain. Kelly had told me they would spend two nights on Mount Hood.

The timing of the trip came up when Kelly was talking about Nikko having only a half sleeping bag to lessen the climbing weight; he still needed a bivy sack to sleep outside. A bivy sack is a nylon, waterproof shell, functioning as a mini-tent for climbers. Kelly's bivy always reminded me of a cocoon.

Kelly told me, "Brian and I have been talking to Nikko. He still doesn't have his bivy sack, and he will need it for the first night on the mountain. But I think he's going to buy it when we get to Portland."

I responded, "I'm sure he will definitely need it since it's December. So I gather you guys are not taking a tent?"

"We decided to all use bivy sacks instead," said Kelly.

"How many nights will you sleep on the mountain?" I asked.

"I'm thinking two nights. Thursday night we will sleep outside in our bivy sacks near our climb and then in a snow cave on Friday. Brian's friend will pick us up on Saturday on the south side and then drive us to the SUV parked on the north side of the mountain."

It is not unusual for climbers to revise their plans. Often when Kelly and Brian returned from a trip, Kelly told me details of how, once there, they decided to shift some logistics or summit timing. They updated their plans based on the weather and additional information they garnered from other climbers who were on the mountain and could provide an up-to-date assessment of the climbing conditions.

I knew this was a smart thing to do, but the addition of another route, in case of an "emergency storm," made me very uneasy. Kelly was a fanatic about studying every detail of a route, and he carefully examined the mountain's topography and pictures of every possible angle. As a landscape architect, he was a master at checking elevations and memorizing natural details and formations. I distinctly remember him sitting on the sofa, staring at a map of the route, and saying to me, "There is no way we are going to climb back down the way we came. I keep looking at this route, and it is way too dangerous to down climb."

His comment took me by surprise, and I responded, "Then how in the world will you get off the mountain?"

Kelly replied, "We are going up and over down the south side. I am not worried about that route. It takes us into Timberline Lodge where Brian's friend will pick us up on Saturday."

Since Kelly had a history of detailing his routes, I wondered why he didn't mention another way down. That didn't sound like him.

At the time, I told Sheriff Wampler, "Something isn't right. Kelly told me that they would spend two nights on the mountain, and he never said anything about another route for an emergency storm."

The sheriff later helped me resolve this question. He explained that based on a conversation with a Nordic skier they met at the Tilly Jane cabin on Thursday, the three climbers were aware of the incoming weather and knew that their timing would be key. They would have to make it up and over on Friday.

Nordic skiers standing in front of the Tilly Jane cabin.
(*Photo retrieved from Kelly's camera found in the snow cave.*)

Oh, I thought. *The weather was not a complete surprise. They revised their plan after they got to Oregon to accommodate the weather forecast.* However, I later learned that while weather reports indicated a change, they did not predict the severity of the storms that were about to hit the mountain. The guys had no idea of what was coming.

Concerned about whether a day climb was possible, I asked the sheriff, "Can it be climbed in one day?"

The sheriff responded, "Oh, yes, it's doable."

But the change in plans didn't stop there. They also made a change regarding where to spend the night. The original plan was to hike in and sleep in their bivy sacks. That's why from the very beginning I was surprised that they spent the night at Tilly Jane, confirmed by the twenty-dollar bill and the thank-you note in the cabin's log book: "We did not plan on staying, but the warmth of the fire changed our minds."

Kelly had showed me a picture of Tilly Jane and explained that at 2.7 miles and more than 5,800 feet in elevation from the ski lodge, they would pass it on the way up.

Staring at the picture of Tilly Jane, he said, "Man, I am excited to see this thing! It has so much history."

Their reduction of climbing time from two days to one would be confirmed by the items the guys stashed in a cubbyhole underneath some plywood sheets at the warming hut. The items clearly indicated they had no intention of sleeping on the mountain. They stashed their stoves, a couple of snow shovels, and sleeping bags. In addition to this gear, they left behind Brian's pack. That way the lead climber would have less weight as he guided the others. In the climbing pictures, Nikko started by leading the climb, and Brian was carrying his pack. The guys wanted to be as light as possible so they could get up and down quickly, shedding almost everything but their ropes and climbing gear.

This is called Alpine climbing. Kelly and Brian were very proficient at it and had done it many times before. They often hid their equipment to lighten their load before a summit attempt. When they climbed in South America, Kelly told me that they had to bury their equipment deep since some of the impoverished children in the town below made a habit of climbing up and stealing climbers' gear. On their way back down they would pick up the gear they had stashed.

Although they had not planned on spending the night at Tilly Jane, they had done their due diligence and investigated the possibility, prior to the trip. I found e-mail correspondence between the climbers discussing the timing if they left from the cabin. Other climbers had told the guys that it could definitely be done in that time period.

ONE PICTURE ON KELLY'S CAMERA WAS OF BRIAN WEARING A BIG GRIN, standing in the doorway of the Tilly Jane A-frame cabin. He was always so happy, and he looked excited to be there.

It was a perfect day for a climb when the guys set out. With no precipitation and temperatures in the high thirties, Mother Nature had delivered a mild winter day, and they were prepared to seize it. But despite their research, they did not have all the facts they needed.

By staying at Tilly Jane, they did not travel as far as they would have if they had stuck to their original plan and bivouacked higher on the mountain. It would be no problem as long as there were no problems.

Little did they know, they had already taken their first step into a brutal encounter with Mother Nature.

As the guys headed out from the cabin, the sheriff believes that they did not get the desirable early start they had intended and that it was not the simple trek they had envisioned. According to him, they probably left between 6:00 and 7:00 a.m., but he thinks they still beat the sunrise on Friday morning.

The sheriff explained to me, "I'm sure they thought they were much closer to the mountain than they actually were or thought that the trip to their climbing point would be easier based on their decision to leave their gear behind."

Part of that gear referenced by the sheriff included snowshoes. They had gone to the trouble to rent them, but at the last minute decided to leave them in the SUV. However, if they were punching through the snow on the trek to their climbing destination, it would take much longer and be exhausting without snowshoes.

Moving beyond the tree line, the climbers took turns leading to break a trail through the snow. Although it was hard work, their spirits rose at they started to approach Eliot Glacier and could see the spectacular beauty of the north face of Mount Hood.

When they arrived at the glacier, they most likely stopped to rope up. It is a common practice for climbers traveling on a glacier to attach themselves together at intervals with a rope to help arrest falls if someone accidentally slips into a crevasse. It was standard procedure for Kelly and Brian because a recent snowfall could easily obscure a crevasse by creating a thin snow bridge that might not hold their weight. Breaking through a snow bridge is something climbers want to avoid at all costs.

While they crossed the glacier, valuable early morning hours were disappearing. Kelly must have thought, *We've got to move faster.* The pictures in Kelly's camera provided vital clues as to the timing and location of the climb. Based on the background light, investigators determined that by the time the guys got to their starting point at the top of Eliot Glacier, it was midmorning.

Now at their climbing destination, the guys were ready to climb the couloirs. The couloirs, vertical gullies covered with ice and snow, run up the center of the north face, with Eliot Glacier below and the summit above. Investigators believe that they decided to climb the left couloir instead of the right one based on time and difficulty. The left couloir is slightly less steep than the right couloir with its harsh sixty- to sixty-five-degree slopes. The north face is considered an advanced route and is usually climbed in late fall and early winter when the snow and ice cover the rocks.

As they glanced up at the north face of Mount Hood, they could see that it was still good climbing weather. Their route should take four to five hours to climb, something that appeared achievable.

According to the sheriff, this too is "totally doable if there are no problems." I felt good that he confirmed that it would still be considered a "doable" climb at that point and the guys even opted for the lesser of the two difficult routes. But I could not escape the comment, "if there are no problems."

While some have second-guessed the guys' decision to climb that route on that day at that time of year, I was sure, from climbing with Kelly and knowing his and Brian's character, that they believed they could tackle it safely. In my heart I knew that the weather must still have been good with no indications of storms at the higher elevations. Kelly knew better than anyone that the combination of a late hour on the summit and bad weather was the kiss of death. The guys were not stupid nor were they on a suicide mission.

Nikko began the climb by leading it, and Kelly snapped pictures. At home Kelly told me that he thought Nikko would lead the climb. I responded, "But you always lead." He explained that while he and Brian had ice-climbing experience, Nikko also had experience and felt very strong in this area.

Other pictures taken farther up the couloir showed that they were into the shadows, meaning the location of the sun was behind the mountain and the day was progressing. As they climbed, it took all their strength, concentration, and will to tackle the near sixty-degree slope with its wicked 2,500-foot drop-off. The climbers were roped together, but Kelly knew that in those conditions, if one of them fell, there was the possibility—even with the protection of ice screws—that all three climbers could be plucked off the mountain.

Every move they made counted, and no one could make a mistake on the sheer icy face. The guys used ice tools and crampons (metal spikes strapped to their boots). They made their way up by swinging their ice tools into the mountain above them and kicking the points of their crampons into the ice below them. As Kelly looked above to their destination, he could see heavy clouds rolling in.

Kelly ice climbing in Colorado in 2006.

At the outset Nikko led the climb, with Kelly in the middle and Brian as the anchor. However, as the climb progressed and the number of daylight hours dwindled, I believe Kelly assumed the lead role. He and Brian were known for being very fast climbers, and time counted. This change in climbing position is supported by one of the photos retrieved from Kelly's camera. In this picture, the climbers' rope is set up in a three-point anchor system, indicating that they were taking the right precautions and protecting themselves against

166

a fall. According to the sheriff, it is not unusual for climbers to take pictures of their setups to later show how technical the climb was. Kelly probably snapped a quick shot to review with Brian and Nikko once off the mountain. The sheriff told me, "I think the significance here is that at this point, they are climbing on solid ice and using a three-point anchor system. This type of setup means they must be on a very steep section and they have ensured that the protection they just put in can support a lot of weight if someone falls." The picture shows no ropes above the anchors, indicating that Kelly was out in front when he took the photograph, a position that would be very consistent with his years of experience. "My guess is that he is leading at this point," added the sheriff.

It was also in Kelly's nature to be assertive if he sensed potential danger, and with more than twenty-five years' experience he had faced almost every circumstance possible. In fact, in the last five years Kelly had become a more conservative climber, putting in more ice screws and pickets (long aluminum bars hammered into snow as anchors). Many climbers refer to this as putting in protection. The lead climber is responsible for embedding this climbing gear into the snow and attaching the rope to brace the climbers in the event of a fall. Brian's size also was a factor in their climbing position. He was usually the anchor in the team, based on his tremendous strength and quick reflexes to steady the group if someone slipped.

As they worked their way up the mountain, the intensity of the climb increased, and Kelly started to get nervous about the incoming weather and the extra time the climb was taking. Then there was a tremendous pull on the climbers' bodies. One climber fell, and all h— started to break loose. At 10,500 feet the unthinkable occurred, and the race for survival was on.

It was at this terrifying elevation, with a 2,500-foot drop below, that investigators believe the accident happened. Based on the climbing equipment left in the snow and the elevation of the last pictures shot in Kelly's camera, this was the point that their quick December getaway became a living nightmare.

Kelly, Brian, and Nikko would have been roped together. Investigators were able to determine that the climbing anchors were properly set and positioned and had done their job, saving the men's lives and keeping them from being thrown off the mountain. But the weight of the fallen climber, combined with the steep icy slope, most likely forced the other two climbers to lose their grips. At 10,500 feet all three men were left twisted and dangling from the same rope.

I AM SURE SHEER TERROR RIPPED THROUGH KELLY, BUT HE WAS ONE OF the most clearheaded people I have ever met in an emergency situation and he would have immediately started to fight for survival. As climbing partners, he and Brian had often talked about this scenario and how they would handle it. In a crisis, each would know exactly what the other was thinking. Despite their new friendship, Nikko, as a fellow climber, would have realized that they must work quickly and apply every survival climbing tactic possible to right themselves and get back into a climbing position to reach safety.

Imagining the guys in this situation was unbearable, but I needed to know the truth of what really happened. When I was mentally strong enough, I called the sheriff a few months after the tragedy. I told Sheriff Wampler, "I need to know." It must be tough for a law enforcement official to have a widow asking for all the details of how her husband died, but Sheriff Wampler never turned his back on my questions. When I asked, he gave me the answers I needed.

The sheriff explained that the self-rescue took a long time, perhaps even hours. *Hours?* I thought, cringing inside. That's an unbelievably long time to be hanging thousands of feet in the air on a mountainside. In addition, it was winter on Mount Hood, and spending hours on a self-rescue would take them into nightfall.

The ordeal must have been brutal on their bodies. But investigators determined that they fought to hang on, and slowly, one by one, the guys were able to right themselves, get back in a climbing position, and start to head up the mountain. But there was a problem with one climber; he was injured and unable to climb on his own. That's when the team decided they needed an emergency place to work from, and the two able-bodied climbers dug a platform. Once on the platform, the two climbers anchored in for safety and started to help the third climber up. Finally, after a tremendous amount of effort, all three climbers were on the platform. They had evaded falling to their deaths and were back together.

As horrific as the scenario was, I had a sense of comfort in knowing that no climber cut the rope of another climber below him to save himself from falling off the mountain. *These were just not cut-the-rope kind of guys.*

The self-rescue had taken a tremendous toll and had claimed precious climbing time. It was dark, and the weather they feared had arrived. The temperature had plummeted, and chilling wind gusts sent shivers through their bodies.

Most frightening of all, one climber was now injured. As the sheriff relayed the facts, I already knew that the injured climber was my husband, Kelly James.

Now that I understood how Kelly was injured, the mystery of what happened next, at the top of Mount Hood, would be answered by additional reports from investigators and from our personal experience of opening the box of Kelly's belongings retrieved from his icy tomb on the mountain.

SIXTEEN

A Box of Clues

I HAD BEEN STARING FEARFULLY AT THE LARGE BROWN CARDBOARD BOX sitting in my living room for two days. It was the box we had been waiting for, but it was also the box we dreaded to see. Based on the postmark, I already knew it contained the items found in the snow cave when rescue workers discovered Kelly's body. The kids and I had decided to open the box together. Ford, Katie, Jack, and Jason and his wife, Sara, had arrived, as had the moment of truth. These items would permit us to have a glimpse of how Kelly spent his last days on earth.

Part of me did not want to look, but another part knew I had to face the truth.

Ford carried the box into the TV room and placed it in the center of the room. We all pulled up chairs around it. I was not the only one who was apprehensive about opening it.

For a few minutes we just stared at it. Then Jack spoke up, "Should I go and get my pocketknife to open this?"

I responded, "That's a great idea."

Then I asked Ford, "Will you please be the one to take things out and show us?"

Ford stood up. He used Jack's knife and slowly opened the box. Immediately we recognized Kelly's red climbing pack, and Ford pulled it out for a closer look. Next he showed us a small brown paper sack.

It took me a second to figure out what it was, and then it dawned on me: *Oh, it's an evidence bag.* I recognized what it was from my former days as a crime reporter when I had watched law enforcement use them. I spoke up, "Guys, since it was an accident, they had to put all of Dad's things into individual evidence bags."

There was complete silence from the kids.

One by one, Ford pulled out the bags and revealed the items. There were small articles of climbing clothing, such as extra glove liners and a lightweight protective jacket shell.

Then Ford pulled out a bag with Kelly's cell phone, the one he used for his last phone call from the snow cave.

Jack jumped up. "That's Dad's phone. Let's turn it on!"

Ford tried to turn it on, but it didn't work.

Jack took it. "It's dead," he said.

"Wait here," I said. "I'll get Dad's charger."

I wondered whether we could get it to work. I had been told that when they found it in the snow cave, it was full of water.

When I returned, Jack eagerly took it from me and plugged it in. I knew why Jack wanted the phone. One day when we were in the car together, I saw him staring out the window. I could tell that he was thinking about Kelly. I asked him, "So what are you thinking?"

Jack responded, "Nothing."

I replied, "You can't be thinking nothing because even if you are thinking nothing, that means you are thinking something." Jack smiled. He had gotten used to me saying this. It was a statement that I repeated often.

Jack paused and then spoke, "Do you think Dad recorded a video message for us on his phone? He showed me how once."

I looked at Jack in amazement and thought, *Never underestimate the thoughts of children.* Even at age twelve, he was trying to put the pieces together of what happened on the mountain.

"Sweetie, I don't know, but that is really smart thinking," I answered. "Dad would be very proud of you." Jack smiled again. I added, "As soon as we get his phone back from the mountain, I want you to check it. Okay?"

Jack enthusiastically replied, "Okay."

With Kelly's long-awaited phone now plugged in and charging, I prayed, *Please, God, he wants to see something on that phone so badly.*

We continued opening the pack, but there were only a few more items and nothing much of interest—only goggles and a small purple bag with his contact lenses. They were items we had seen dozens of times in the past.

And then Ford stopped.

I asked, "What else is in there?"

"That's it," he said.

"What do you mean? That can't be it," I responded.

"There's nothing else," he said.

I instructed him, "Check the bottom of the box."

But there was nothing.

Kelly had taught all of us how to climb, and we understood that it was not what was in his pack, but what was missing from it that mattered. There were no sleeping bag, pad, bivy sack, stove, fuel, or food. None of the essentials he needed to survive.

I was overcome with sadness and thought, *He didn't have a chance. But I know he fought like h— to hang on.*

The reality of what happened in the snow cave was sitting in our TV room.

It was so overwhelming that none of us could speak. We all just sat there for fifteen minutes in total silence, staring and crying at the sight of Kelly's gear now lying on the carpet. Then we realized that his ice tools were missing.

He might not have had the essentials to fight off the sub-zero-degree temperatures, but we knew Kelly had to have his ice tools because they were his lifeline to getting off that mountain.

The two ice tools found on the snow platform had to belong to Kelly. That was confirmed by the sheriff's earlier statements; because the ice tools were exactly the same, they were believed to have belonged to one climber.

We knew who that climber was.

AGAINST THE ODDS KELLY, BRIAN, AND NIKKO HAD SURVIVED THE FALL. They were now seeking shelter on the snow platform from the raging storm and regrouping about what to do next.

Every man had to be silently praying, *Please, Kelly, don't be seriously hurt,* too afraid to say the words out loud. Getting hurt high on a mountain can be a death sentence. No one knew that more clearly than Kelly. He often read assessments of climbers' fatalities to learn from their mistakes, but when it came to injuries, he just shook his head and said, "Many times climbers don't stand a chance if they are injured in high altitude." That thought had to be crossing his mind.

First up for the guys was to assess Kelly's injuries. There were visible signs of injury on his legs; they were scraped and bloodied when the climbers fell. Investigators later viewed the abrasions as those consistent with a slide. But another troublesome injury was not visible. In the accident, it is possible that Kelly also suffered a severe injury to his right shoulder.

Initially the sheriff indicated that he believed Kelly had a shoulder injury, but that was disputed in the media when they reported that the autopsy showed no injuries. I was always skeptical and thought even if Kelly had dislocated his shoulder, he would have snapped it back into place on his own. It was something he had done in the past when he wrestled in high school. Kelly had an incredible pain threshold.

My belief that he had a shoulder injury was later confirmed by his death certificate, which stated, "Other *significant conditions contributing to death,* but not resulting in the underlying cause given above: Possible right shoulder dislocation."

With Kelly injured, the climbers went into rescue mode. They had already survived this far. Together they could make it. They believed if they could get off the snow platform, climb a little higher, and reach the summit, they could go up and over to the less technical south side or down the Cooper Spur route as referenced in the climbers' note.

But what about Kelly? Brian and Nikko could not leave him on the snow platform. While it served as a temporary shield from the fierce winds, it was not enough shelter for a whole night.

Together all three climbers devised a plan on how to reach the summit. They started to cut the rope to make an ingenious support system to help Kelly up the mountain.

AS I THOUGHT ABOUT THE GUYS CUTTING AND TYING THE ROPE, MY MIND wandered back to another Friday night that I spent with Kelly and Brian. Kelly told me that Brian was coming over for steak and we could all watch a movie together. That sounded like a great idea. After a good dinner, we gathered in the TV room to watch the movie. What the guys had forgotten to tell me was that it was a video about how to tie climbing knots. Brian had come prepared with two twelve-inch pieces of rope and handed one to Kelly. He then said to me, "Sorry, I forgot to bring you one." I sarcastically replied, "That's okay. The fun is watching you guys do it."

The video provided close-up shots of a pair of hands tying dozens of different climbing knots. I told the guys, "You have *got* to be kidding. This is how we are going to spend Friday night?"

They started howling with laughter, and Kelly said, "Come on, baby. I'll get you a piece of rope. It will be fun."

"That's okay," I said. "You guys knock yourselves out and have a great time."

They could not stop laughing because they knew it was a boring video, but they were truly excited to tie knots all night. Kelly responded to me, "But, babe, it's only 8:30 p.m."

I said, "I know, but somehow bed is looking a bit more exciting than watching you guys tie knots all night."

That was then, and this was now. I started to cry. I missed them so much and could actually visualize them working on that snow platform.

WITH DARKNESS ALL AROUND, THE GUYS USED THEIR HEADLAMPS TO CARRY out the rescue mission. All three climbers, shivering in the frigid temperature, sat on the platform. During the time they were dangling from the rope and working with all their might on a self-rescue, the weather continued to worsen. The precipitation began with rain and evolved into snow. Because of the lengthy period it took to recover from their fall, the guys were not able to escape the weather. They were now wet and the coldest they had ever been in their lives. As the sheriff had said, "The climb was doable if there were no problems." But there had been a major problem.

On the snow platform it seemed to be getting colder and colder, and it was not their imaginations. The temperature was plummeting. It was a far cry from the mild near-forty-degree temperature they had experienced hours before when they left Tilly Jane.

The guys knew they had to work quickly and get out of there as fast as they could. Together they used all the climbing survival techniques that they had ever learned and devised a rescue tactic that was resourceful and amazingly effective. They cut sections of rope and tied themselves together so they could walk three abreast, putting Kelly in the middle. Nikko and Brian could support him as they climbed to the summit. It's an unusual climbing technique, but accident scene photographs show three sets of tracks walking horizontally from the anchor at the snow platform to the summit.

Just prior to leaving the snow platform, Kelly glanced down at his two ice tools and knew they were of little use. It had to be a tough realization for him since a climber's equipment is his lifeline to survival. He could no longer survive by himself, and he needed the help of his two buddies. Brian and Nikko had no plans of abandoning him.

As they left the snow platform, the guys were confronted by the vicious winds that they had temporarily escaped. Making their way to the summit under such conditions was something I believe that very few other climbers could have accomplished. But they were phenomenally strong men, physically and mentally. They had gone that far together, and they had no intention of giving up. It must have been terrifying, but the bond of the climbers gave them superhuman strength to survive.

Side by side, they forced themselves to forge on. Chipping away slowly, they moved up the face of the steep icy slope. Estimates are that they were being slammed by wind gusts up to fifty miles per hour, resulting in sub-zero-degree temperatures. The temperatures were making it almost impossible to use their ice tools. Their hands were stiffening up from the bitter cold, and the weather was getting worse. They had no idea that it was just the beginning of the worst storm to hit the mountain in more than a decade. Due to the blowing snow, the climbers could not even see what was in front of them, but they knew what was behind them, a 2,500-foot sheer drop. Stopping was not an option. Once again Kelly thought, *Got to go up. Got to get off this north face.*

In more than two decades of climbing, it was the most brutal climb of Kelly's life. The climbing was excruciatingly slow. But finally their efforts paid off. They were at the summit. His spirits rose as he thought, *Now we have a chance.*

They had reached the top and a way of escape. At least that's what they initially thought.

However, the brief flash of hope was almost immediately extinguished. On the mountaintop they found whiteout conditions with raging winds up to one hundred miles per hour. The winds were blowing so hard and so much snow was whipping around them that it was impossible for one to hear what the other was saying. They motioned for everyone to move forward. They needed each other to push on in the extreme weather conditions.

They headed south a short way but soon realized that finding shelter was more important. The risk from exposure was death. The guys could barely stand. It seemed that the wind was targeting them, trying to knock them off the summit. One wrong move could result in all of them taking a disastrous fall to their deaths.

It was clear that they would have to abandon both plans, either to descend the south side or to take the Cooper Spur route. In addition to the high risk from exposure, the visibility was so bad they could not see which way to go. The weather had concealed all the landmarks and routes that Kelly had studied so diligently before this climb. The only thing that they knew for sure was that if they didn't act quickly, they would die.

Andrew Siegel

In this close-up shot taken from the air, the black dot near the center is a rock and the snow cave is directly below it. The formations in the snow that look like sagging wet paint are caused by blowing snow and steep terrain, which make the avalanche threat very high.

They thought their best option was to drop back down southeast of the snow platform to get out of the wind and seek shelter. Time was of the essence. The decision was made to descend three hundred feet above the Newton-Clark Glacier on the east of the north face, where they started their climb, and build a snow cave to escape the hellish situation. They clearly understood that it was incredibly dangerous, but they were forced to go down the only route they knew. They were survivors fighting for their lives.

The guys secured their ropes and descended from the summit by lowering themselves until they reached an area by a rock. At that location, they anchored in, and Brian and Nikko dug frantically to make the snow cave for the three of them to huddle together. The weather continued to bear down on them. After they finished digging a hole in the snow big enough for all of them, they helped guide Kelly into the cave. He was in excruciating pain, but he tried to conceal it. He told himself, *I'll be fine in the morning.*

Amazed that they had survived, the guys were out of the vicious weather and were able to think more clearly. They were still alive. Kelly knew that they had to get off the mountain, but was uncertain at this point how they would do it.

They chose to hunker down for the night and make a decision in a few hours. Perhaps Kelly would regain his strength and the trio could make it down together.

While in the snow cave, rest seemed impossible, though. The beginning stages of hypothermia were taking hold on all three climbers. It was a sleepless night. Kelly thought about his warm bed back in Dallas and how Karen would always reach out and make sure her foot touched his when they slept. For the first time, the mountain was his enemy. It brought no sense of peace but only tremendous pain and anguish. Kelly was homesick and desperately wanted to be with his wife and children.

SHORTLY BEFORE 4:00 A.M. ON SATURDAY, DECEMBER 9, THE CLIMBERS discussed their options for getting off the mountain. After weighing their choices, they agreed on the best way to retreat. Then Brian and Nikko asked Kelly the question he dreaded. Kelly reluctantly responded, "I can't do it. You will have to go down without me." Brian's heart sank. It could not be happening. The two men were more than climbing partners; they were brothers who swore they would never leave each other on a mountain. It was the hardest conversation of their lives because their lives depended on it. Brian always needed Kelly, and Kelly needed Brian. For the first time on a climb, they would be forced to separate.

Brian and Kelly on the summit of Denali in 2001.

Kelly understood it was the right decision, but he was tormented by the fact that he physically was unable to do something that he had done dozens of times before, descend a mountain.

But I believe Brian probably had the toughest time. He would do anything to save Kelly's life. I knew it the first time I met him five years ago when we all had dinner together. And today, I still believe their unwavering commitment to each other lasted until the very end. The two men had been through life-and-death situations before, and they had always survived together. Both Brian and Kelly were convinced that the only solution was for Brian and Nikko to descend and get help.

Brian and Nikko left the snow cave in the predawn hours of Saturday morning, unlike their late start on Friday morning. Before they left, I am sure Nikko joined them in something Kelly and Brian did routinely before a climb. Together they bowed their heads, and Kelly led them in a prayer for God to protect their descent from the mountain and to watch over their families.

As the guys stood up to leave, Kelly had confidence that they would soon be back with help. As tough as Kelly was, he never had a problem expressing emotion, and I am sure that he turned to Brian and said, "Love you, bro."

But then he would have added his own Kelly James touch to their departure by saying something obnoxious just as they headed out.

Any one of Kelly's close friends would confirm that it would not be out of character for him to leave them with these parting words: "Hey, guys, I won't be there to save your sorry a— if you fall. So pull up those pretty pink panties of yours and get down off that mountain safely. Hey, and don't forget to bring me a brewsky when you come back."

But Kelly's story was not over. He would tell us more about his final days in the snow cave when we turned on his cell phone.

AFTER A COUPLE OF HOURS, KELLY'S RECOVERED PHONE STILL WOULD NOT charge up. The older kids called it a night. We said good-bye to them, and just before climbing the stairs to bed, Jack and I decided to try one more time. Jack pushed the on button, and this time the phone responded. We both sat down eagerly on the kitchen floor to see what it could tell us.

Immediately Jack went to the video section. Kelly had not recorded anything for us. Then he went to the pictures, but there were no new pictures. Upon reaching the text messages, Jack said, "Dad didn't open any of these." As he went slowly through them, I was reminded of how diligently the sheriff's department and all the rescuers had worked to try to locate the three guys.

The first text message was on Saturday night, December 9, from Brian's friend who was scheduled to pick them up earlier that afternoon at the base of the south side of Mount Hood. It read, "Hey, didn't hear from you, so I got a room down the hill. If I don't hear from you by 10 am [on Sunday] I will call for help."

The next series of text messages started on Monday at 4:51 a.m. I thought it must have been after they were able to triangulate his call.

The first text message read, "This is Hood River 911. If u recv'd this message, please reply." An identical message was sent two minutes later.

Less than an hour later, they sent another message: "This is Hood River 911 tx if u get the tx msg."

If their plan was to text every hour, I could tell the person texting was getting anxious as the time intervals between sending messages became shorter. The next message was sent forty-five minutes later. It read, "R u injured reply yes or no."

Less than ten minutes later, they sent a message of hope: "Please reply when you get this. Help is on the way."

It would be noon before the last and final text message was sent: "We are trying to find u do u have a gps? If so what r ur coordinates? We believe we know where u r within 3 to 4 miles. Storm is setting in. God Bless Kelly!"

As I fought back the tears, Jack proceeded to the missed calls button on the cell phone. The last recorded numbers belonged almost exclusively to the kids as they dialed their dad's number again and again in hopes he would answer.

The last incoming call was from me on Wednesday morning, December 6. Kelly was already at the airport, and I had just dropped Jack off at school and was calling to say good-bye again and wish him luck.

To my surprise, the outgoing calls were the ones that sent me reeling. There were a total of nine outgoing calls with the majority not making it out due to lack of cell service. The first call was on Wednesday, December 6. Kelly called me at 6:42 p.m., and we talked about his climb the next day. Each said, "I love you."

On Thursday afternoon, he had tried to reach me twice. He said he would try to call me on Thursday but didn't think he could get a call out because of bad reception. Even though I did not get the call, I knew Kelly had tried. We had always done everything we could to make sure we never went to bed without saying, "I love you."

The next call was to me at 3:52 a.m. on Saturday. I wondered why he did not try to place a call on Friday night. My question was quickly answered. One minute later, he placed two calls in a row to 911. My stomach sank and I started to cry. My husband had tried to call me just before 911. He knew he was in trouble. The timing of the calls indicated to me that they ran into trouble late Friday afternoon. Kelly did not call on Friday night because they were still trying to get out of the fierce weather and into the snow cave.

I believe he called me when Brian and Nikko left early Saturday around 4:00 a.m. to go for help. The 4:00 a.m. hour fits timing about when the other two climbers might have chosen to venture out and descend the mountain. Once alone, Kelly would have tried to call. I wondered whether he placed that call to 911 to tell them that Brian and Nikko were on their way down.

It all sounded right and in keeping with what Kelly would have done.

The next two calls Kelly placed were to 911 later on Saturday at 2:22 p.m., but neither went through.

There was no activity until almost twenty-four hours later when Kelly must have heard his phone ring. I am sure he was shocked. He had been trying desperately to reach me and 911, but no calls were going in or coming out. After hearing his phone ring and missing the call, he was able to push redial. His last outgoing call was to Jason, Ford, and me on Sunday afternoon. We would talk for a precious six minutes and forty-two seconds.

It seemed strange to me that only two calls made it out. Ironically the call to me on Wednesday, December 6, was at 6:42 p.m., and the length of time for the last call on Sunday, December 10, was 6:42, six minutes and forty-two seconds. The numbers 6-4-2 appeared on the phone log for the first time and the last time we talked on the mountain.

On Saturday, Brian and Nikko left Kelly in the snow cave to descend the mountain. Investigators found two definite sets of tracks going away from the cave. They led directly down the mountain to a dead end above an area known as Black Spider above the Newton-Clark Glacier. The tracks then headed back up the mountain to the north toward the top of the Cooper Spur route where they said they would descend if something went wrong. Then nothing: no visible tracks could be found. It is believed that on Saturday as they were trying to descend, Brian and Nikko fell victim to the vicious weather and were possibly swept off the mountain by the hurricane-strength winds or lost their footing and fell thousands of feet into a crevasse below. Despite an extensive search by ground and air, the snow and vast mountain terrain prevented investigators from finding any more signs of the two climbers.

HAVING KELLY'S CELL PHONE AND STARTING TO PUT TOGETHER THE TIMING of the tragedy were too much for me. I asked Jack to go upstairs and get ready for bed. I would be there in a minute. I walked into Kelly's office and dropped to my knees. My heart felt like it was breaking all over again. Even though it was after 10:00 p.m., I picked up the phone to call Jessica. She knew what the family and I planned to do that evening.

When I heard her voice, I started sobbing and said, "He tried so hard to reach me." I could tell she was crying on the other end. She and her husband, Robert, also loved Kelly, and all of this seemed like a bad dream. I needed to hear the strength in a girlfriend's voice. After talking for a few minutes, I was able to gain my composure, thank her for talking to me, and tell her I loved her. Then I hung up the phone.

Wiping my eyes, I walked upstairs and went to Jack's room. He could tell I had been crying, so I explained, "I'm sorry, honey. Seeing the calls on Dad's phone made me sad."

Jack looked lovingly at me, nodded, and said, "You know since I am only twelve, I don't want to die right now." The way he said it almost made me laugh because it was so matter-of-fact. He followed up: "You know I am not afraid to die because I am so excited to see Dad."

My heart melted. I smiled and said, "Me too, honey."

I kissed Jack and turned out the light. I was so proud of him and my husband. I can't remember one night when Kelly was home that he failed to pray with Jack. Kelly stood up in a dramatic fashion, reached out into the air, and pretended to grab something. He then thumped his fist on Jack's chest and said, "Ask for Jesus to come into your heart." The thump always sounded so loud, and I could hear Jack laugh across the house. After that

Kelly and Jack prayed and talked about God. Kelly taught Jack about heaven, and now his teachings were paying off in ways that I never could have imagined. *What more of a gift can a parent give a child?* Jack believed beyond a shadow of a doubt that, through his faith, he and his dad would be together again. This time, I cried tears of joy.

I thought about how much I loved Kelly and wished he could be with me to tuck Jack into bed. Before heading to my room, I ran back downstairs to get Kelly's blue climbing jacket that I had picked up at the funeral home earlier that day. I felt the tremendous need to sleep with it. I so desperately wanted to hold him, and curling up with his jacket was the closest I could get. As I closed my eyes, I held the jacket tightly and asked God, *Please tell me this didn't really happen.*

SEVENTEEN

Finding Kelly

IN MY HEART, I BELIEVED I KNEW EXACTLY HOW KELLY SPENT HIS FINAL DAYS, but it would be one year after Kelly's death that I finally gained enough courage to call the rescue worker who found him dead in the snow cave. It was time for me to learn if my beliefs about what I thought happened actually did. Soon the details around Kelly's last minutes, hours, and days would no longer be a mystery, and I would learn that my first instincts were correct. With death, God had not severed our bond of love and my deep understanding of my husband.

I already knew the name of the rescue worker who discovered Kelly, and I reached out to Captain Chris Bernard to connect us. Captain Bernard assured me that pararescuer Joshua Johnston would be glad to speak with me. Within a couple of days, Josh and I had a memorable phone conversation.

Curious about this young man who found Kelly, I asked Josh to tell me about himself. Twenty-five years old at the time of the rescue, Josh joined the air force's pararescue division after high school, and he became proficient in sky diving and mountain and rock climbing, using these skills to conduct helicopter rescues in the water and the mountains. This experience gave him paramedic training, which led him to his current undergraduate studies in premedicine and his plans to attend medical school.

When the Mount Hood search began, Josh was splitting his time between college and the 304th Rescue Squadron out of Portland. He was certainly no rookie to rescues or the fallout when things did not go according to plan. We were not the first grieving family Josh had spoken with. Prior to finding Kelly, he had already seen more than his fair share of death with two tours in Iraq and one in Afghanistan. In fact, while he was serving in Afghanistan, the helicopter in front of Josh went down and crashed, killing all on board. Josh was on the scene and tasked with identifying the casualties. Lying dead in the wreckage was his best friend and fellow pararescuer.

While he talked about his background, my mind drifted to a time Kelly and I were standing in the airport, waiting to go on vacation. Across the terminal, a group of soldiers wearing sand-colored camouflage fatigues and carrying duffel bags had gathered. Kelly told me, "Wait here." He proceeded down the concourse until he was in the middle of the group. I watched him shake hands, slap the troops on their backs, and talk as if they were long lost friends.

About ten minutes later Kelly returned, and I asked him, "What did you say?"

"I just told them how thankful I was that they were protecting us and I realized the sacrifices they are making."

He was a huge fan of the men and women who defend our country day in and day out. He said many times that while he had very few regrets in life, one of them was that he never joined the military.

Listening to Josh's background, I knew Kelly would be impressed with this young man, and I thought, *If Kelly were here, he would love to talk with this guy and listen to stories about rescue missions all night long.* He was exactly the person who was meant to discover Kelly.

While the 304th Rescue Squadron was involved in the search from the beginning, Josh joined his team a few days later, since he was in Florida on standby for the space shuttle launch. As part of his pararescuer duties, it was standard procedure to be out of the state and on standby in case his services were needed.

After the shuttle launch, Josh flew back to Oregon and joined his fellow pararescuers from Portland. Saturday, December 16, was their first flight up the mountain since extreme weather conditions had prevented them from making an earlier rescue attempt. From the air they spotted the climbers' abandoned gear and a depression in the snow. But it was getting dark, too late for a rescue. They had to return to the command post, regroup, and plan for a drop on the summit on Sunday.

Josh Johnston

The search and rescue team that found Kelly includes members of the U.S. Air Force Reserve's 304th Rescue Squadron, Portland Mountain Rescue, and the Hood River Crag Rats. Josh Johnston is on the left.

The next day, the 304th Rescue Squadron met in Hood River with the National Guard unit out of Pendleton, Oregon. The unit had flown in its CH-47 Chinook helicopter. Josh explained that with the helicopter's twin engines, it is a powerful machine with the ability to steadily hover between seventy-five and one hundred feet over the summit.

After participating in a morning mission briefing, Josh, four other pararescuers, and two members from the volunteer rescue group, the Crag Rats, took off for the summit of Mount Hood. At the summit, the rescue workers prepared to be lowered one by one by a hoisting cable. Wearing climbing harnesses, they clipped into the cable and left the safety of the helicopter. Once on the summit, each rescue worker anchored himself to keep from being blown off the mountain by the snowy wind of the rotor wash. It was a slow process, but with each successful descent, Josh knew they were one step closer to finding the missing climbers.

It was a relief to finally have nice weather, and the rescue workers quickly went into action to find the rope anchor and the depression in the snow with tracks leading away from it, which had been seen earlier from the Chinook. In the world of search and rescue, spotting such evidence is considered a huge achievement for an air crew. The rescuers' ability to locate this scene from the air once again confirmed their expertise and talent. For more than a week, dozens of incredible people had dedicated themselves to finding these three all-American guys trapped on Mount Hood and it was now time to bring them home.

It didn't take the rescuers long to locate the depression that, surprisingly, turned out to be a snow platform rather than the cave they were expecting. After finding the platform empty of climbers but filled with evidence, the searchers spread out to look for other clues and followed existing tracks. But Kelly's snow cave was proving to be very difficult to find. The rescue workers searched all day, going up and down, back and forth, on lines secured to anchors at the summit. After coming up empty, the rescue team decided to do one more search before calling it a day.

That was when Josh had an idea.

During an earlier team search, they discovered a couple of tracks that didn't seem to lead anywhere, located about a quarter of a mile away from where the climbers' gear was spotted. The tracks were near a snow-filled field at a sixty-degree angle on the mountain's north face. The climbers' gear was located on the other side of the snowy field.

Josh thought it was worth a shot. He lowered himself three hundred feet off the summit in the location of the snowy field. Looking up toward the summit, all he could see was a steep sheer face of snow. But then something caught his eye. It was a three-foot black rock sticking out of the snow. Josh thought, *On this part, it's the only place someone could go.*

He made his way toward the rock, calling out for the climbers. At the rock, he started to gently swing his ice axe like a wand, hoping he could find evidence of the climbers. Then he tapped his ice axe and took one swing into a large lump of snow. A section of snow fell off, and Josh knew he had found the entrance to the snow cave. It had been covered up with a couple of inches of snow that had drifted over it. Against the odds, the rescuers had found what they had been searching for.

Todd Wells/Crag Rats

Rescue workers looking for Kelly's snow cave.

"It was a quite a surprise to find it, and the odds were very small. It's a huge mountain and it was lucky," said Josh.

Upon entering the snow cave, he could see Kelly lying on his side, facing the entrance of the snow cave.

Josh immediately started yelling, "Hey, are you okay? Are you all right? Is anyone else in here?" He could tell the cave was big enough for three climbers, and he wasn't sure if someone else was in there. When there was no response, Josh's first thought was that Kelly might be unconscious, but upon examining him, he realized the rescue would not have a happy ending.

He took a step back and became a bit confused. It almost appeared that Kelly was making a rude gesture. "At first, I thought he was giving me the bird," said Josh.

Taking a closer look, Josh realized that Kelly had taken off one of his gloves and curled back all his fingers, except for his ring finger that prominently displayed his signet ring.

Josh remarked, "I think it was symbolic." He told me that Kelly had an incredible, peaceful look on his face, and he believed Kelly knew he was going to die and tried to provide a last sign to comfort the family.

His words rang true in my heart, and I believe that Kelly's faith and his trust in God provided this peace. Upon his passing, Kelly was no longer trapped between heaven and earth.

In addition to his last act, Josh commented that Kelly had obviously kept his wits and done everything he could think of to survive by placing all his belongings between his body and the snow, trying to fight off the hypothermia as long as possible.

"I've done the training, and people who are in a hypothermic state and able to do all the things they need to do to stay alive are amazing. There was no misstep with Kelly," explained Josh.

As Josh further described Kelly's condition, I fell back into my wifely role and asked, "Did he eat his orange?" Kelly told us on the phone the last time we spoke that he only had an orange to eat, and I had often thought about how hungry he must have been.

Josh paused as if trying to remember, then responded, "Oh, yes, there were orange peels in the snow cave."

And then I asked the toughest question of all: "Josh, when do you think he died?"

He responded, "I believe that he had to have been dead at least the night before we got there, but there is a possibility that he was still fighting the day before."

Kelly's death certificate places his death within three days of the hypothermia setting in, saying he died of prolonged exposure. As painful as it was to hear Josh's assessment, I believe that he was right, and due to Kelly's fighting nature, he survived longer than his death certificate indicated.

It was getting difficult for me to talk through the tears. I thanked Josh for his time and everything he had done. Just before we hung up, I said, "I am really happy that God picked you to find him."

Josh paused and replied, "Thank you."

It was then that I realized that finding Kelly's snow cave had never been a sure thing, and it had only become a reality because of Josh's hunch.

EIGHTEEN

Discovering Peace, Purpose, and Comfort

UNDERSTANDING WHAT KELLY WENT THROUGH PHYSICALLY ON THE MOUNTAIN was only half of what I was searching for in order to come to terms with his death and find a sense of peace.

I thought about what happened to him emotionally as he was stranded in the snow cave facing the brutal sub-zero-degree temperatures. I was fortunate enough that in our relationship, Kelly and I had many long, meaningful discussions about our faith, death, and why God put us on earth in the lives that we have.

There were many things that I admired about my husband, but his comfort level with dying definitely set him apart. Kelly was not scared to die because he had no question regarding his destination. Based on our previous conversations about heaven and God, I had a strong belief that I understood his dying thoughts, but I was still hoping to find physical proof on his cell phone after they recovered it in the snow cave.

Although there were no cell phone messages or scribbled notes on a piece of paper tucked away in his backpack, Kelly did not let me down. It turned out that he did leave behind the exact thing that I needed to find peace.

While cleaning out his file cabinet a few months after his death, I came across a small notebook lodged in the back under a metal flap. I had never seen it before. Upon opening it, I immediately recognized the handwriting and knew I had stumbled across Kelly's private thoughts. They provided a wonderful raw glimpse into his thoughts about climbing and death. One of his writings read:

> I love life, I enjoy what God has given me &
> I grab it with both hands & pull life into my heart.
> I have seen true beauty, most people never experience.
> Thank you Father, I recognize this is not possible apart from you.
> I cannot resist the lure of adventure, I crave it.
> I'm absorbed by challenge, & to a certain extent, Danger.
> Thanks for your protection!
> I am motivated & driven to climb more now than ever,
> even at the expense of death.
> Death has no hold on me & does not instill fear in my bones.
> I do want to live, but not at the expense of being idle.
> I know God wraps his loving arms around me
> & cradles me in his palms.
> I know I scare my family and friends
> but I don't want to live unless I can live.
> I think everyone understands reluctantly.
> I just want to enjoy God's beauty with his help.
> HE IS MIGHTY!

For Kelly, climbing was like breathing; he *had* to do it. I was grateful to have discovered his personal writings, and I found peace in reading and rereading them. Doing that brought me some comfort, but I was still trying to understand God's purpose behind his death and my life going forward.

Kelly's life had tremendous purpose. He brought incredible love and spiritual enlightenment to me, the kids, his other family members, and his friends. But I had to open my eyes wide to see any possible purpose behind his death. At first, I couldn't see anything but pain resulting from the loss of a father, husband, son, brother, and friend.

I understood that things happen here on earth that we will never comprehend, but I still wanted to associate some positive things that resulted from the climbing tragedy. Based on the letters I received from perfect strangers and the number of people who stopped me on the street with tears in their eyes, as if one of their own family members had just died, I knew Kelly's story made an impact.

Through family members' and friends' interviews with media who covered the story of the missing climbers, I believe that the world got a glimpse of three adventure-filled men who loved life, their families, and God. For some people the guys were proof that Christianity is not just for soft-spoken, rule-following, near-perfect men. Kelly was far from perfect. But he was always striving to be a better man. He was a guy's guy, who freely shared his faith, never fearful that others would see it as a weakness; rather, it was an incredible strength. Even in my grief, I was able to see that God used this tragic event and our suffering to reach out to people.

In addition to thinking about God's purpose surrounding Kelly's death, I wondered about my purpose as a widow. Many nights, I asked God, "So what do You want me to do now?"

One day while I was contemplating my future, I said to God, "Hey, look, this is the worst thing that has ever happened to me. So if You are going to use it for Your good, let's go for it. Use me and use me in a big way because I need to feel some sense of purpose with all that has happened."

It was the first time that I had ever truly wanted to work for Him, despite the consequences to my life.

The topic of God's purpose came up in our Bible study just prior to Kelly's leaving for Mount Hood. Our small group was talking about how we can maximize our time here and let God use us for bigger things. Kelly was invigo-rated during our talk while I just nodded my head. I knew how I should be responding, but quite frankly I winced at the thought of any significant change in my life.

When our guests left for the evening, I went into the laundry room to wash clothes. The meeting was over, but I still needed to make sure that God understood my thoughts on the subject. I had read enough of the Bible to know that people who got heavily involved with God did not always have a foo-foo and fairy dust life here on earth. Spiritually we reap the benefits in heaven, but truth be told, I was enjoying my current life and praising Him on my own schedule.

I stood in my laundry room and said, "God, I know I agreed with every-one in Bible study, but I really don't want You to use me right now because I am very happy and thankful for my life. If You use me, I am afraid You will take something away."

To this day, that conversation with God haunts me. He would soon show me that as a loving parent, He decides how, when, and what we will face in life. God knew that the biggest fear in my life was losing Kelly.

It was what I feared most, and it happened.

But I never thought that He was punishing me. In time I would under-stand that He wanted Kelly with Him and He wanted me to carry on in a new direction. It is a role I would be forced to have without Kelly.

During this painful time, I was very aware that God was all around. Each day I received some level of comfort to be able to make it through the next twenty-four hours.

The recognition of "blessings in sorrow" came after a shift in my mind-set. It was sparked when I remembered an interview I had seen several months before the tragedy. I was watching Larry King, and he was interviewing Pastor Rick Warren, author of *The Purpose Driven Life.* I can't recall exactly how the conversation went, but I do remember what I took away from it. Larry was asking Rick about dealing with the highs and lows of life. Rick responded something to the effect, "Larry, I used to think that life was a series of highs and lows, but I have come to realize that with the lows there are always good things that are happening."

It was my turning point.

Remembering this conversation changed my whole perspective on losing Kelly. That was the lowest point of my life, but I felt convinced that if I started to look for some good things, I would see them.

And it happened.

Instead of dwelling on what I lost, I decided to focus on what I had.

Then amazing things occurred. I was given blessing after blessing. Some of them were small by our worldly standards, but huge for my journey of faith.

One blessing came in the realization that Kelly's death was not a random act. As I reflected on all that had happened, I could not shake the feeling that despite the chaos, there appeared to be some kind of bizarre order to what had happened. I replayed the events again and again. The similarity was so strange between my great-grandfather being an architect and climber and Kelly being a landscape architect and climber. It was ironic that Kelly had died almost nine years to the day I met him, and that the first time he told me "I love you" was on a mountain and the last time he said those words he was on a mountain.

I wondered if it was just intuition that I told the sheriff to look for his JKJ ring for identification, and Kelly had extended that exact finger before he died. In fact, even after talking to Josh Johnston about finding Kelly, I did not get the full impact of what my husband had done in his dying act until I saw it for myself. Unaware that photos of Kelly in the snow cave existed, I naïvely asked the rescue workers to send their search and rescue pictures. After receiving several CDs, I inserted them into my computer and started clicking through the photos. Within several minutes, I stopped cold. It was a click of a mouse I will never forget. Suddenly on my screen was a shot of Kelly's hand with his ring finger extended. I could not move or breathe; it was the most powerful photo I had ever seen. I now understood why rescuers told the story of him sending a signal. Just as Kelly approached life boldly, he died the same way and had extended his arm and hand in a way that no one could mistake was a signal.

I sobbed as I looked at the pictures of Kelly in the snow cave, and I spent the next two weeks reliving the ordeal with nightmares that did not leave me in the morning when I opened my eyes. Despite the pain of seeing the photos, I was thankful because I knew with all my heart that something very special had happened as he lay two miles in the sky and I was below telling rescuers to look for his signet ring.

Another remarkable thing that I could not put out of my mind was our last phone call. I know that he was trying to reach us before that call. Why, then, did the phone just happen to get through when the boys and I were together trying to locate him? As the weather worsened on Mount Hood, it's hard to believe that the weather cleared at the exact time the boys and I tried calling Kelly so we could update the sheriff who was waiting for feedback on whether to launch a rescue.

I also couldn't forget the bizarre sensation of warmth that ran through my body on the Wednesday night when we were in Mount Hood. While it remains a mystery, I know something happened that I cannot explain.

THE EVENTS IN OUR LIVES LEADING UP TO THE INCIDENT, THE ACCIDENT itself, and the things that happened afterward started to make me wonder and believe even more deeply that life is not a series of accidents strung together. As I connected the dots, I also started experiencing small things that seemed a little out of the ordinary. While some might say it was just the wishful thinking of a grieving widow, I can tell you that I received comfort in a time of deep sorrow. Fortunately my girlfriends were there to experience quite a few of these "coincidences."

One memorable incident happened while I was out to dinner with six of my girlfriends. It had been a challenging period for quite a few of us in the group, and we were lending our ears and support as only true girlfriends can. We had a great conversation, and I was so thankful for their friendship. Dinner was over, and the waiter passed around a plate of fortune cookies. I was the last one to take a cookie. In the tradition of fortune cookies, everyone started opening hers and reading aloud the fortune inside. Everyone else read aloud the traditional fortune cookie language we have come to expect. As I broke mine open and read the piece of paper inside, I blinked to make sure I had seen it correctly.

Written on the back of my fortune was "Miss You." The front read, "Those with imagination and not learning, have wings not feet." I thought, *Yes, honey, you now have wings. You had so much imagination, but despite all those close calls, the lure of the mountain was too great to learn from the near misses that one day you might get into a situation that you couldn't get out of.*

When my friends asked me about my fortune, I read it to them. They immediately responded, "No way."

I passed the slip of paper around the table to prove I was not making it up.

As I sat back in my chair, I smiled and whispered under my breath, "I miss you too."

It was just a preprinted saying on a piece of paper, but the coincidence of the wording seemed odd. Ironically I later found two crumbled up fortunes in Kelly's wallet retrieved from the snow cave. He put the fortunes in his wallet after a special dinner we had together. His fortune said, "Your vibrant personality inspires others, stay that way." Mine read, "God will help you overcome any hardship."

I was also fortunate to share these special connections with the kids. A couple of days before Katie's twenty-first birthday, I was working in Kelly's office, which had become my home office. Throughout the day, I had an incredible nagging feeling to go through a file drawer of his papers. I had looked in there before. The papers were just work-related, nothing I considered of real importance.

Finally in the afternoon I gave in to the nagging feeling and went through the papers one by one. After about five minutes, I saw something that surprised me. It was a piece of paper that said, "To My Princess." Princess was Kelly's pet name for Katie. The piece of paper was a beautiful happy birthday love poem to her. He had written the poem three years ago and filed it away. When I read it, I started to cry and could not believe what I had in my hands. The next night I took all the kids out for Katie's birthday and gave her the poem. I told her, "I found this in your dad's office. I don't think he wanted to miss being here for your twenty-first birthday." Both of us started to cry, and she said, "I can't believe you found this. I remember him doing this, but I didn't have a copy. I can't tell you how much this means."

Other things made us laugh and cry at the same time. In one instance, my girlfriends and I were out for dinner. I was the only red wine drinker at the table, so they ordered me a glass of merlot. When the waitress came back, I asked, "What is this? It's really good."

"Climbing," she replied.

I was stunned and thought she might be playing a cruel joke. "Excuse me. What did you say?"

None of my girlfriends could speak. They were just staring at the waitress.

"Climbing, the wine is called Climbing Merlot," she said.

We all started to laugh, and I said, "What are the odds?"

There was also the time that I was handed a bottle of private label water from behind a store counter when a woman said, "Looks like you could use some water." The label clearly read, "From Mount Rainier." I just shook my head. It was the mountain where Kelly and I were engaged.

Another strange incident happened after I had been home a couple of months from Oregon. My mother called me one morning and said, "Karen, do you remember that bag of bulbs I handed you when you were at my house the day you learned that Kelly was missing?"

"Yes," I responded.

"Have you planted them yet?" she asked.

"No, Mom," I said. "I haven't really been in the mood to garden."

She then paused and said, "Well, I want to tell you something before you look in the bag."

Nervously I asked, "What?" I didn't like the tone in her voice, but at the same time I thought, *It's just a silly bag of bulbs.*

She explained, "You know that I did not know what mountain Kelly was climbing when this happened?"

"Yes," I said.

She went on, "Well, I don't want you to get upset or think anything bad when you look in the bag. You see, I gave you my favorite daffodil bulbs to plant in your garden and that type of bulb is called 'Mount Hood.' You will see it on the tags inside the bag."

I was silent a few seconds. "Mom, that's weird."

"I know," she said. "I've hesitated to tell you, but I didn't want you to be surprised."

I said, "Thanks for telling me. I love you." As I hung up the phone, I wasn't quite sure what to think.

Looking back, I believe these were gifts from God as He watched over me and gave me hope. As I reflect on everything I have encountered—from dreams lost to a renewed belief in mankind and strengthened faith—I believe now more than ever that there are no coincidences and that there is a grand plan in which we all play a role.

I have witnessed God putting the perfect people in my life at the perfect time, just like a beautifully conducted orchestra. I have been blessed to see His hand at work, and I take great comfort in knowing that it was no mistake that I have been privileged to have the most wonderful friends and family to stand by my side during the good times and the bad times.

One of my dear girlfriends wrote me a note with words that touched my soul. She said, "Yours is a blessed life, a beautiful life and an enduring love story."

Despite all that has happened, her words are true. I have been blessed to really understand what it is to love and be loved. I do not question why God decided to take Kelly. I have faith that for some reason He has left me standing with a clear direction to carry on.

ON WEDNESDAY, AUGUST 22, 2007, KELLY CAME HOME TO ME IN MY dreams. It was the longest dream I can remember, and it seemed so real. When Kelly entered the house, we walked around together and talked about everything. I updated him on the family and kids. We talked about how hard it had been for me without him. We discussed how I was taking care of the house, down to details pertaining to cleaning the outdoor hot tub. We spoke of our love; we were so lucky to have known each other.

For one night I felt I was married again, and when I woke up, I thanked God for my dream. I realized that God had given me another blessing. Throughout my life, I thought making memories was about doing big things that leave an impact.

Now I know that in the end what you really remember are the little things such as enjoying the sunset together on the deck or walking around the garden to see the plants blooming. These are the moments of which dreams are made.

What I didn't understand before the loss of Kelly was that love truly transcends death. I believe that when our souls connect in love and through faith, the ones who go before us never really leave our side. If I remain still enough and pray for God to comfort me, I am filled with the wonderful, memorable joy of my husband's love.

This connection was extremely strong on the one-year anniversary of Kelly's death. We marked it with a candlelight remembrance for all three climbers. Katie and I spoke of our love for Kelly and God. Michaela, Nikko's wife, sent words of appreciation and a prayer request that her husband and Brian would be found. While Brian's dear friends paid tribute to him at the service, his sister, Angela, sent her love as she lit candles at the base of Mount

Hood during the time of our remembrance in Dallas. Once again the families were united and stood strong in their love for the climbers and each other.

For us it would be our second Christmas without Kelly, and in true James family style, we stuck together like glue and honored the man and the baby born in a barn who had enriched our lives beyond words.

WITH ANOTHER NEW YEAR APPROACHING, I WAS SEARCHING FOR SOMETHING to lift my spirits. *What would Kelly tell me to do?* Then suddenly it hit me: *Paint!*

Before Kelly's death, my art was gaining attention with gallery showings in Dallas and Santa Fe, but I stopped after Kelly's death.

Then a story I had completely forgotten came flooding back to me. The day before Kelly left for Mount Hood, he suggested that I continue to develop a new style I had started. The new style of painting was a heavy texture piece, and when Kelly originally saw it, he said, "Look at all the footholds. It looks like something I would rock climb."

I remember laughing and thinking, *Is* everything *about climbing?*

But Kelly wasn't the only one who loved the painting; Brian did too. One evening, Kelly greeted Brian at our front door and said, "Man, you have got to come upstairs and check out her new painting. It's great!"

Brian's comments were very complimentary. Ironically a friend of his ended up buying it as a surprise and gave it to him just before he and Kelly left for the mountain. Kelly was so excited that his dear friend was in possession of one of my best paintings.

As I remembered this story, my confidence grew, and I dusted off my paint brushes. I spent the next couple of days preparing several canvases and started applying layers of texture. I decided that was how I was going to spend New Year's Eve. It would be me, the cat, a bottle of wine, and my art, and I was very happy with this plan. I had gracefully turned down kind offers to spend the evening with several couples. While I knew I was growing stronger in my relationship with God and gaining peace with what happened, I was still a bit socially timid and thought I would be better off staying home and painting.

That evening while I busily worked on my art, I noticed something strange on four of the canvases. I had just applied a white sealer, so I could not understand where all the red paint was coming from. I checked my hands because I had used my fingers to smear on the sealer. It was not paint, but blood. The texture was so rough on the canvas that it cut my fingertips. As I stood back, I thought, *Getting to this point really has been about blood, sweat, and tears.* The blood-smeared canvases seemed appropriate at the outset of another new year.

My joint art exhibition with Denver Moore in May 2008.
Left to right: Ford, me, Jack, Denver, Katie, and Ron Hall.

Despite my journey onward, make no mistake; the tears still flow. These are not the same tears that I once shed on Mount Hood, however. The emotion now comes from gratitude for the love that I experienced. I take great comfort in knowing that one day I will be reunited with my husband. I have no fear of death, for I know Kelly will be there to greet me and take me by

I draw a heart and write Kelly's name in the sand in May 2007,
five months after his death.

the hand. I have been blessed to experience love so deep that I know it transcends death and I will never walk alone.

For me, the worst tragedy of my life enlightened me that holding fast is the only way to live. I believe that when Kelly died, God still had a purpose for us as a couple. Kelly did the first part, and now it is my turn to step up, hold on strongly to my faith, and share the incredible joy I have received from knowing that God is in control and still loves me when I stumble. Although bad things happen, God is always good.

When the question was posed, "Where was God on Mount Hood?" I knew the answer immediately.

God was everywhere.

He was in the snow cave with Kelly.

207

He was wrapping His arms around Brian and Nikko as they ventured down that mountain.

He was comforting us during their disappearance and through the painful realization that He was taking them home.

He was protecting the rescue workers as they battled the brutal weather to search for the guys.

He was lifting up my friends and family and giving them incredible strength to help take care of me.

Yes, God was everywhere.

As Kelly James would say, "HE IS MIGHTY!"

PART 4

A Legacy of Love

The Greatest Love Affair

AFTER KELLY'S DEATH, I WENT IN SEARCH OF EVERYTHING THAT HE HAD ever written to me. I was so thankful that I had taken the time to carefully tuck away his love letters and poems during the years we were together. One afternoon, I curled up and started to reread the stack of papers to recapture those feelings when I first realized the depth of his love for me.

While reading his writings, I noticed that in the majority of them, I was not the sole character. That had never been apparent to me before. Kelly also included his love for God; there had always been three of us in this love affair.

I was so thankful that God had given me the eyes to see what I had missed the first time I read Kelly's writings. I wondered whether in heaven Kelly was just shaking his head and grinning from ear to ear, saying, "*Now* she gets it." While I thought my faith was very strong at that point, I was quite ashamed of myself for thinking it was all about *me. Did Kelly know I missed this very important message in his letters?*

Kelly was instrumental in my walk with God, and I desperately missed our long talks about our faith and our role in God's plan. In fact, I missed this so much that after Kelly's death, instead of talking about God, I started talking to God and I entered into a relationship with Him like none I had ever dreamed existed. Without my earthly mate to talk with throughout the day, I found myself in constant conversation with God from the moment I woke up to the minute I closed my eyes at night. He was more than my Maker: He was my friend, my comforter, my strength, and the reason I got up in the morning. After all, He made me and I am still here. He has to have something in mind for me.

Over time, I gained a sense of clarity and peace. From our worldly standards, the Bible's admonition to "embrace your trials" seems counterintuitive, but Kelly's death and my dependence on God led me to understand this concept. It is perfectly stated in 1 Peter 1:6–9:

Now for a little while you may have had to suffer grief in all kinds of trials. These have come so that your faith—of greater worth than gold, which perishes even though refined by fire—may be proved genuine and may result in praise, glory and honor when Jesus Christ is revealed. Though you have not seen him, you love him; and even though you do not see him now, you believe in him and are filled with an inexpressible and glorious joy, for you are receiving the goal of your faith, the salvation of your souls.

Kelly James once said to me, "I would die in a heartbeat to save souls." Back then, I didn't understand because I had my eyes fixed on this earth. With my eyes now on heaven, I understand why my husband made that statement, and I am very proud to say that I was not the greatest love of his life. That honor belongs to Jesus Christ.

Love Poems from Kelly

God is with us
We are in his hands now
God is with us
Peace & happiness, our gift
God has put us together
We are one
My heart beats strong for you my love
We are one
You are my love & you are my wife.
Your Husband

Helpmate

If my steps are slow
& my heart weary . . .
If I fall behind
Please wait for me
I will wait for you . . . my darling
Should I fall behind
Please wait for me . . .
Should I cry, wipe my tears,
When I am weak, hold me tight,
Should I stumble, give me a shoulder
You are my helpmate

Marriage

Turmoil, strife, confusion
We live our lives

God = love, truth, confession & comfort
We live our lives

Courage, strength, belief, & faith
Our thread to love & happiness

My mate, my love, my wife
Together we stand convicted

Our universe seems so small
But God understands it all

We have each other
We have each other
A comfort & blessing to be sure

Ours is to live
Together we love . . . and . . . hope . . . and . . . live . . . & struggle
But ours is to live

Letters Left Before Climbs

My Sweet Karen,

I can't tell you how much I Love You & what you mean to me.

Your love & concern & commitment to me have fulfilled a peace in my heart that no adventure could ever fill.

Thank you so much for always being there for me no matter what. I will always be there for you too.

I am so happy God has blessed me with your love & companionship. What a beautiful day each day is knowing I have you in my life.

I Love You,

Kelly

Holding Fast

To My Dearest Sweetheart:

Know that I am with you always.
You are the sunshine of my life.
Thanks for making my life complete.
My world is so fulfilled now that you have become my wife.
Thank you for your help with the kids & all the good advice you give me;
I really do listen.

I will truly miss you & I'll be thinking of you on the mountain when I'm in
    my tent,
I'll be thinking of you when I'm trudging through the snow,
I'll be thinking of you when I've got both ice tools embedded in the ice,
I'll be thinking of you when I straddle the summit,
I'll be thinking of you when I get back in my warm sleeping bag,
I'll be thinking of you when I'm hiking down through the village,
I'll be thinking of you in Huaraz &
I'll be dreaming of coming home to you when I'm in Lima.

Thanks for putting up with me & my crazy trips.
Relax & take time for yourself, I'll call when I can.

Know that I love you always sweetheart.
Love, Kelly

Climbing Scrapbook

Kelly climbing Alpamayo in South America.

Kelly's view of the steep drop from the top of a mountain in the Andes.

I love you princess
Dad

Kelly and his daughter, Katie, before a climb on Mount Rainier.

Friends and family on Mount Rainier.
Left to right: Sean McCarthy, Ford James, Brian Hall, Jason James, Kelly, and Paul Burton.

Kelly and Brian with their hair and beards frozen after a climb.

Kelly at the summit of Denali.

Acknowledgments

I HAVE WITNESSED GOD PUTTING THE PERFECT PEOPLE
IN MY LIFE AT THE PERFECT TIME, JUST LIKE A BEAUTIFULLY
CONDUCTED ORCHESTRA.

TO MY FRIEND BRIAN HALL: YOU WERE A PART OF OUR FAMILY, AND WE MISS
you tremendously. Thank you for caring so deeply about Kelly. I know you
are now safe together climbing a magnificent mountain in heaven.

To Dwight, Clara, and Angela Hall; Michaela Cooke; and Maria Kim: we are
bonded in a way that very few can understand. Thank you for all your love and
support. I look forward to the day we are reunited with our three climbers.

To an incredible team who made this book possible and helped me fulfill
my purpose: I will never forget the friendship and dedication of my agents,
Dan Johnson and Bucky Rosenbaum, along with Joel Miller, Kristen Parrish,
D. B. Kellogg, Heather Skelton, Jennifer Greenstein, Walter Petrie, Kristen
Vasgaard, and the other wonderful people at Thomas Nelson who believed
in this project.

To my family and Kelly's family, who were always there in the darkest of
times and listened no matter what the hour: I could not have made it

through without the love of my mother, Ann; my father, Roy; Nancy; my brother, Karl; Deborah; Dylan; Jason; Sara; Ford; Katie; Jack; Lou Ann; Frank; and Traci.

To our dear friends who watched over me in Kelly's absence: I know that he, too, is very thankful for the kindness and love of Kathleen and John "Jake" Jacobson; Jessica, Robert, and Alexa Nuñez; Ellen and Steve Miller; Tina Stacy; Donna Eagan; Gretchen Gerlach; Ken Malcolmson; Barbie Lowe Geri; Ashley Blaker; Bill Palen; Dana and Chris Hanks; Karen Boulle; Doug Black; Jody Baker Monahan; Chris, Katherine, Caroline, and Claire Millet; Russell McKown; Keith Airington; Donna and Cliff Welch; Dave and DeAnn Stewart; Daniel and Vicki Rodriquez; Sean McCarthy; and Bryan Weber.

To all the churches across the country that prayed for us and our guys and helped us along the way, most notably Fellowship Bible Church of Dallas and our pastor, Gary Brandenburg; Park Cities Baptist for opening its doors; and Riverside Community Church of Hood River for its words of comfort: your prayers lifted me up to carry on.

To my former employer, Fleishman Hillard, who extended love, Elaine Tasker for her research on my family history, and Camille Liebbe for helping feed our family when we returned home.

To the incredibly kind people of Oregon who donated countless hours of their own time and resources to help us find Kelly, Brian, and Nikko. I know I speak on behalf of all the family members when I say a tremendous thank you to all of you who voluntarily put your lives on the line or supported those who did. There are so many names and groups to list. If I neglect to mention anyone involved, please forgive me. Thank you, too, to the entire Hood River County Sheriff's Office, and to Sheriff Joseph Wampler and Deputy Matt English for helping me with the book; Air Force Reserve's 304th Rescue Squadron, Captain Chris Bernard, and Staff Sergeant Joshua Johnston for all that you did; Dave Waag, Todd Wells, and all the Crag Rats; Steve Rollins and the other members of Portland Mountain Rescue; Clackamas County Sheriff's Office; Oregon National Guard's 1042nd Air Ambulance Company; Eugene Mountain Rescue;

Acknowledgments

Corvallis Mountain Rescue; Mountain Wave Communication; Federal Bureau of Investigation; Oregon Snowmobile Association; Nordic Ski Patrol; Nevada Air Guard; Hood River Airport; United States Department of Agriculture—Forest Service; ARACAR; Silver Star, Cooper Spur Ski Resort; Hood River Hotel; Mount Hood Meadows Ski Resort, and T Mobile; and to the Hood River area retailers that donated food and supplies: Shortt Supply, Starbucks, Wal-Mart, Safeway, and Les Schwab Tire Center.

CPSIA information can be obtained at www.ICGtesting.com
Printed in the USA
LVOW07s1912291213

367275LV00010B/46/P